"The most logical, commons(approach I've ever heard."
—Zig Ziglar

"[Bill Staton's] book really opened my mind and got me started on the path to stock investing. I couldn't put it down."
—Thomas Winninger, CSP, CPAE,
CEO, The Winninger Companies USA

"Bill provides a simple plan anyone can use to begin building an estate and at the same time build their own self-confidence right along with it. Buy a copy for yourself and some others to pass along to people you care about."
—Jim Cathcart, author of *The Acorn People* and *Relationship Selling*

"As [Bill Staton] promised on the program, getting started was incredibly simple and required minimal time."
—Bill Michaels, 97X Radio, Davenport, Iowa

"I can see where financial advisors would want to have [Bill Staton] shot at dawn because [he has] taken concepts that they try to complicate and made them easy to understand."
—Al Walker, CSP, CPAE

"Every American must put the achievement of financial independence on the front burner. Bill's book will show you how to do it quicker, faster, and easier than any other investment strategy ever known."
—Brian Tracy, author of the best-selling
Maximum Achievement

"Bill Staton is an inspired investment guide who makes the process more fun than you ever guessed. But the real fun comes in seeing your results from Bill's straightforward instructions."
—Eugene Dickson, President, Leslie Advertising

"Bill takes textbook material and makes it as entertaining as a novel."
—Ty Boyd, CSP, CPAE

"*The America's Finest Companies Investment Plan* is one of the finest treatments of investing with the divinity of simplicity."
—Cavett Roberts, CSP, CPAE

"[Bill Staton makes] a Tremendously confusing subject Tremendously simple."
—Charles E. "Tremendous" Jones, author of the best-selling *Life Is Tremendous*

THE
AMERICA'S
FINEST
COMPANIES®
INVESTMENT
PLAN

1998 EDITION

THE AMERICA'S FINEST COMPANIES® INVESTMENT PLAN

1998 EDITION

Double Your Money
Every Five Years

Bill Staton

NEW YORK

Excerpt from *The MONEY Book of MONEY* by Robert Klein, 1987;
copyright © 1987, Time, Inc. Reprinted with permission.
Excerpt from "Beware: Tax Consequences of Mutual Funds," reprinted by
permission of *The Wall Street Journal;* copyright © 1992 Dow Jones &
Company, Inc. All rights reserved worldwide.
Brealey's chart from *An Introduction to Risk and Return from Common
Stocks* by Richard A. Brealey. Copyright © 1969 by The Massachusetts
Institute of Technology. Reprinted by permission of The MIT Press.

Copyright © 1995, 1997, 1998 Bill Staton

Foreword copyright © 1998 Mark Victor Hansen

All rights reserved. No part of this book may be used or reproduced in any
manner whatsoever without the written permission of the Publisher.
Printed in the United States of America. For information address
Hyperion, 114 Fifth Avenue, New York, New York 10011.

"America's Finest Companies®" and "The Staton Institute^SM—America's
Finest Investors®" are registered trademarks of The Staton Institute, Inc.

ISBN 0-7868-8264-6

10 9 8 7 6 5 4 3 2

The author gratefully acknowledges permission for use of the following:
The quotation from H. Bradlee Perry appears courtesy of H. Bradlee
Perry: The Babson Staff Letter, published by David L. Babson and
Company, Inc.
"The Equity Premium: Stock and Bond Returns Since 1802" by Jeremy J.
Siegel. Adapted, with permission, from Financial Analysts Journal,
January/February 1992. Copyright © 1992, Association for Investment
Management and Research, Charlottesville, Virginia. All rights reserved.
"A Conversation with Benjamin Graham" adapted, with permission, from
Financial Analysts Journal, September/October 1976. Copyright 1976,
The Institute of Chartered Financial Analysts, Charlottesville, Virginia.
All rights reserved.
SRC Century-Plus Chart of Investment and Economic History® courtesy
of Securities Research Company, a Division of Babson-United
Investment Advisors, Inc., 101 Prescott Street, Wellesley Hills,
Massachusetts 02181.
"Where America Was a Century Ago: History as a Guide to the Future"
by John Center. Reproduced, with permission, from The Futurist,
published by the World Future Society, 7901 Woodmont Avenue, Suite
450, Bethesda, Maryland 20814.
Dividend Reinvestment Plan statement courtesy of Public Service
Company of North Carolina, Inc.
Earnings and dividend ratings for common stocks used by permission of
Standard & Poor's, a division of McGraw-Hill, Inc.
Excerpt from The Intelligent Investor, Fourth Revised Edition by
Benjamin Graham. Copyright © 1973 by Harper & Row, Publishers,
Inc. Reprinted by permission of HarperCollins Publishers, Inc.
Excerpt from Where Are the Customers' Yachts? by Fred Schwed, Jr.
Copyright © 1940 by Fred Schwed, Jr. Copyright renewed © 1967 by
Harriet Wolf Schwed. Reprinted by permission of Simon & Schuster,
Inc.
Excerpt from "A Closer Look at Mutual Funds" from Fortune, October
7, 1991, appears courtesy of Fortune, © 1991 Time, Inc. All rights
reserved.

To me there is no greater wealth than being blessed with a wonderful family. I dedicate this book to my lifelong partner, Mary, and our four incredible children, Gracie, Tate, Whitney, and Will. You have my heartfelt gratitude for enriching my life so often and in so many ways.

CONTENTS

CONTENTS

FOREWORD

Dear Friends:

Bill Staton is an entrepreneur's entrepreneur. If you would like to earn money, save money, and have your money multiplied, then listening to Bill Staton is one of the wisest things you could do. He is the next Warren Buffet. He has created a system that never fails to generate profits that are growing, safe, and fun to watch. He uses the highest principles of money management. Bill teaches them with exquisitely simple forms, and he initiates you into money mastery.

After I listened to Bill's tapes, I said to my nine- and eleven-year-old children, "Daughters of mine, here's what we're going to do with your investment money." They looked through my copy of *America's Finest Companies* and picked the companies they think are winners—companies such as Microsoft, Intel, Hershey's, and General Electric. The bottom-line question I asked them was, "Are people going to need more computers and more silicon chips, eat more chocolate, and use more electricity in the future than they do right now?" Their investments over time have continued to grow and multiply. I believe this will make them financially free and independent.

Bill's material excited me at the fiber of my being. I have shared this information with my family, my writing partner, and my staff because the simple truth is that it works, it gets results, and those results get you further results. You have to invest only about one hour a year in an effortless plan to become financially free and independent. You start with a little and end up with a lot. When you put in more, you'll end up with more. These are the wonderful principles of compounding and masterly money management—practical, simply communicated, and so well done that anyone can execute them.

It is my dream and hope that everyone in America becomes aware of Bill's elegantly simple principles so that America can become debt-free and financially independent. We need to have a brighter, more exciting, and more enriching tomorrow than we've ever had before.

MARK VICTOR HANSEN
Co-author of the #1 *New York Times* best-selling series
Chicken Soup for the Soul

CHAPTER ONE

Why You Should Invest in America's Finest Companies

In the big book of things people more often do wrong than right, investing must certainly top the list, followed closely by wallpapering and eating artichokes.

—THE MONEY BOOK OF MONEY, 1987

M aking your money work for you ought to be fun and easy, safe and sure. You don't have to be a professional or spend every waking moment to build funds for your future. You don't have to take a lot of time from your own career and personal life. And you don't have to hand your money over to one of the more than 9,000 mutual funds.

Investing isn't voodoo or hocus-pocus. The word *invest* comes from the Latin *investire*—to commit for a long period with the thought of future benefit. To invest means to put money to work today so that it will earn more money for the future. You invest your money in something to reap a profit.

Investing (as opposed to speculating and taking unnecessary risks) is a process. A process is a series of actions leading to an end. By definition, then, investing is something you should start now, or should have already started, and plan to continue indefinitely. Stocks are the best—and the easiest—asset to invest in.

During my twenty-six years as a money coach, I've learned that individuals can get the most from their money just by following a few simple guidelines. My investment program is built around America's Finest Companies, and will show you how to be your own money manager. There is no Wall Street jargon, there are no complicated rules, no complex formulas, nothing to buy. Everything you need is within these pages.

I'll explain in plain English how the stock market works—why certain principles apply and a lot of others don't. I'll show you that stocks have provided a higher return than any other investment, including real estate, for more than a hundred years. You'll learn what it takes for a company to be in America's Finest Companies and why these companies have far outdistanced the stock market. You'll also learn the simple process of investing for maximum profits with least risk.

America's Finest Companies is compiled once each year and is eagerly awaited by my newsletter subscribers and the financial media. That's because these companies are the elite of corporate America—the top 3 percent of all public companies—with at least ten straight years of higher earnings or dividends per share.

You wouldn't go to the racetrack and bet on the nags, would you? That would be a sure way to lose money. Doesn't it make sense, then, that your hard-earned dollars, the dollars you're accumulating for your children's college education, a larger home, another car, retirement, or whatever, should be invested in shares of the finest companies you can buy? If you wouldn't bet your money on nags at the racetrack, you shouldn't bet your money on companies that aren't proven winners.

Building and managing your own "mini-mutual fund" picked from America's Finest Companies will take very little time—one or two hours per year—and allow you to outperform 75 percent of the pros 100 percent of the time. This is the best way I know to reach your financial goals. It's even better than investing in mutual funds. Why? Because America's Finest Companies deliver spectacular returns.

Since World War II, a diversified portfolio (group) of stocks has grown at 12 percent compounded annually, a higher return than from any other investment. Just by earning 12 percent each year, you'll regularly outperform 75 percent or more of all professional money managers. But you should be able to earn more than that—13–15 percent annually—with a diverse portfolio chosen from America's Finest Companies. That doesn't sound much better than 12 percent, but, assuming you invest as little as $2,000 per year for thirty years, the 1–3 percent difference will be worth an additional $120,000 to $460,000.

This is an easy-to-read-and-understand guide to making

money with the cream of American companies. Anyone can dramatically improve his or her financial health with my time-proven, powerful method, which is deceptively simple to implement. There are no gimmicks or tricks. A young person can begin to invest with as little as $300 and easily become a millionaire (even a multimillionaire) well before retirement.

Let me share with you the wonderful story of Florence Gray, the proverbial "little old lady" who amassed an estate worth $2.5 million. And guess what—she never earned more than $9,000 in any single year.

Florence Gray was a market researcher who passed away five years ago at age eighty-nine. She accumulated almost her entire fortune by using simple, sane principles of long-term investing, the same ones I emphasize over and over again in these pages. In 1924, Ms. Gray made $19.27 a week in her first job.

Remembered as a stickler for details, she was a numbers cruncher before computers were born. She had a talent for tracking down information on market and population trends. Her boss talked her into putting money into stocks, and she took the plunge with gusto by speculating (taking a huge risk) with borrowed money (buying on margin) just before the Great Depression struck. Learning a great lesson in how to lose a lot of money the hard way, she switched to buying highest-quality companies and never again strayed from the course.

Florence Gray didn't go to college, and unlike most Americans today, she knew exactly where her money went. She didn't spend it unless she had to, but she was fond of traveling to Europe and did so on several occasions. She favored companies with rising dividends, and after retiring she invested all the money from her Social Security and pension checks and lived off her dividends. The bulk of her portfolio at death, not surprisingly, was in America's Finest Companies: Smucker, Merck, Society Corp., Consolidated Natural Gas, and Exxon, to name five.

Her attorney, Ed Hack, summed up her winning philosophy very simply, "Over the course of time, she managed to invest in equities for the long haul and stuck with them and rode the winners. She was not supporting an extravagant lifestyle, and it just began to compound." Florence Gray, I wish we'd known you.

One cardinal principle holds true: By buying only the shares of high-quality companies, you'll become a successful investor. You'll be part owner of companies that are in sound financial condition, that won't go out of business, and whose earnings and dividends will continue to grow.

A company must earn money to remain in business. Otherwise it will eventually go bankrupt. Part of those earnings are paid to investors in the form of cash dividends. The rest is plowed back for research and development; to bring new products or services to market; to buy new, more productive equipment; to hire more employees. All earnings put back into the company enhance the value of the business. As the value of the business rises, so does the price of the company's stock. It has to.

One excellent example of a company that's done a superior job enhancing the value of its business—and its share price—is Wal-Mart Stores, one of the brightest lights in America's Finest Companies. Wal-Mart is among a handful of companies with more than thirty consecutive years of higher earnings per share. Through the end of 1996, Wal-Mart had thirty-five straight years of rising earnings and thirteen of higher cash dividends paid out to owners of its stock. Since 1985 revenue skyrocketed from about $8.5 billion to more than $105 billion in 1997. The share price exploded twelvefold from $3 to $36.

Wal-Mart and its founder, the late Sam Walton, are practically household words, as are a lot of America's Finest Companies—Coca-Cola, Clorox, DuPont, Exxon, Johnson & Johnson, Merck, and Sara Lee, to name a few. But there are just as many that are totally unfamiliar to most people, whether they are investors or not. For example, there's The Washington Real Estate Investment Trust. Ever heard of it? I hadn't either until seven years ago.

Washington REIT—you guessed it—invests in real estate. It prides itself on being maverick, unorthodox, and conservative. The company mails some of the most interesting annual and quarterly reports to shareholders. These reports tell how the company is doing. A 1993 quarterly noted the company moved out of its old headquarters (after selling it for a tenfold profit) into the basement of its new WRIT Building. I've never before seen a company press release about abandoning offices with windows for offices without. But Washington REIT isn't your typical enterprise. In early 1993 the company burned its last outstanding mortgage in the company stove and toasted a few marshmallows in the process. To be on the safe side, they asked the building fire marshal to stand by with a fire extinguisher, and they also mailed a press release about this extraordinary event.

Washington REIT does more than mail witty notices to the press and its shareholders. It earns lots of money. By the end of 1996, the company had put together a total of fifty-seven years of higher earnings and dividends per share, a record just twenty-three other public companies (out of more than sixteen thousand) can match. Ten thousand dollars invested at the beginning of 1971 is worth more than $1 million today. That's a record few other companies or professional money managers can match.

If you want to begin your own investment program, you can quickly name ten or twelve financially sound companies whose earnings or dividends will continue to grow well into the future. How do I know that? Because everywhere I have led a workshop on investing, I've asked the audience to choose a portfolio of five to eight companies. In every instance to date, they've picked high-quality companies in a variety of industries. The majority of the companies they pick are in America's Finest Companies. That is, they have at least ten years in a row of increasing earnings or dividends per share, establishing them as the top 3 percent of all public companies.

Of course, you may be thinking, "Why should I be in stocks at all? They're too risky. Look how far they fell during the Crash of 1987—23 percent in one day. That was worse than in the Great Depression. I wouldn't own any stocks. I couldn't sleep at night if I did."

If you're thinking that, you're not alone. The most frequent comments I hear about stocks and the stock market are negative. (I use the terms *market, stock market,* and *market indexes* interchangeably. They mean the same thing in the investment world.) Here are a few I've heard in my seminars:

"High risk/high reward." (the emphasis is always on high risk).

"Frothy." (picture a rabid dog foaming at the mouth).
"A bottomless pit."
"Extremely volatile."
"Too complicated."
"A loser's game."
"Only an expert should try it."
"Like walking down a dark alley in a crime-infested neighborhood."
"I'd rather visit the dentist."

I do hear positives, too, but they're normally about as few as friends in a cobra pit. It's been like this for the twenty-five years I've been in the investment field.

Let's suppose you'd been in my office in December 1979 asking me what you should do with your money in the eighties and nineties. I would have said, "You should invest all the money you can in stocks, but first there are a few things you ought to know.

"An actor will become President of the United States and will preside over the biggest budget deficits in the nation's history. The deepest recession since the 1930s will occur in 1981–82. Nearly 20 percent of the workforce will be unemployed at some point during that period. There'll be another recession in 1990–91, in which that high percentage will again be without jobs.

"The biggest crash in stock-market history will occur in fall 1987, followed by a 'crashette' of huge proportions two years later. And oh, by the way, there'll be war in the Middle East with the United States leading the charge. A new plague—AIDS—will crop up around the world, plus there'll be record droughts and floods and some record-shattering hurricanes, too. There will also be a collapse of the dollar, scattered depressions in various states, a record number of personal, bank, and S&L bankruptcies, alongside numerous criminal convictions on Wall Street.

"Crime will appear virtually out of control in many major cities, and a riot in Los Angeles will turn out to be the most expensive in history. Some of the largest corporations in America will lay off employees ten thousand at a time.

"Now, do you still want to buy some stocks?" Your answer, most likely, would have been a resounding "No." Yet that would have been a bad answer. Between 1980 and today, stocks outperformed bonds, stamps, Treasury bills (roughly the equivalent of a savings account), diamonds, oil, gold, housing, the cost of living, Chinese ceramics, farmland, foreign currency, and silver. Stocks as a class were by far the number-one investment. Shares of America's Finest Companies were even better. There was no close second.

If you picture investing in stocks as buying pieces of paper that go up and down in value every day like yo-yos, I understand why you might be hesitant about owning shares of any companies. But you don't have to look at them that way. A better viewpoint is that you become part owner of one or more of the finest businesses in this country.

My guess is that if you had enough money, you wouldn't mind owning all of Coca-Cola or Wal-Mart or Exxon or Tootsie Roll Industries or Colgate-Palmolive or Procter & Gamble or McDonald's. You know they're well-established corporations with superior credentials. You also know that year after year their earnings and dividends will continue to grow, and you have no reason to suspect they won't remain viable for as long as you live and even for decades after that.

At this point, you might respond, "But what about companies like General Motors and IBM? They used to be among the best companies in America, but then had so much difficulty in recent years. Their stocks collapsed. I don't want to go through the agony of seeing one of my stocks fall from 176 to a low of 41 the way IBM did."

My answer is "I'll show you a foolproof technique in Chapter 7 that will allow you to make substantial profits in any environment—including the Great Depression—as long as you invest in companies that don't go out of business. Both GM and IBM, even though their share prices gave up a lot of ground, are still in business, so you could eventually make money if you own them. But America's Finest Companies doesn't include either because they don't meet my strict requirement of subsequently higher annual earnings or dividends."

Even though you don't have the billions of dollars it would take to buy a Wal-Mart or PepsiCo and make it your own, you do have enough money to buy a few shares of one, if not both, of these companies. Those shares, or pieces of the business, represent your proportionate ownership of Coca-Cola, McDonald's, or whatever else you buy. They're great businesses to own parts of, and they're bound to increase in value over the long term—the next five, ten, fifteen, twenty years, or more—because the values of their businesses are growing every year. That hasn't been the case with GM and IBM.

By assembling a portfolio of at least five companies in America's Finest Companies, each in a different industry, and adding to the portfolio on a regular basis (preferably annually), you should regularly double your money every five to six years. That's far faster than from any other investment.

By investing only in corporate thoroughbreds, you can take a lot of worry from your shoulders. You can quit worrying about inflation, interest rates, government legislation, recessions, etc., and how they will affect your investments. Since you're only going to invest in the best American industry has to offer, you can let the companies do the worrying for you.

Think of yourself barreling down a river of white water like the Gauley in West Virginia, which has the fiercest rapids east of the Mississippi. I've rafted the entire length of this beautiful river three times. You have to cross the world's largest earthen dam to get to the foot of the Gauley. It's extremely intimidating to look well over a hundred feet down at the treacherous water gushing through the chutes at the bottom of the dam. The roar of the water pushing through is so loud it's hard to hear anyone talk.

I was mildly terrified (all right, I was scared to death) the first time we put our raft into the water, despite the fact I knew we had a reliable guide to get us safely through the roughest parts. Contrary to what I thought, the most dangerous part of white-water rafting isn't shuttling through the turbulent rapids. It's other people clowning around with the paddles and hitting one another in the face. The next most dangerous thing is trying to stand up in the fast-moving shallow water and getting a foot caught under a rock. That's an easy way to drown.

The Gauley River isn't menacing when you know what you're doing. Buying shares of companies in America's Finest Companies isn't menacing either because these companies know what they're doing and have proven it over the past ten years or longer. They know how to circumnavigate problems in business and the economy and take maximum advantage of the opportunities. Placing your money on a portfolio of them is as sure a bet as you can make. Two hundred years of American investment history proves that.

As "America's Money Coach," I am a trainer, an instructor, an investment guide. I am not a drill sergeant. I coach people to manage their money themselves, to take charge of their financial affairs, and to achieve financial security. I learned what I know the hard way.

Having graduated from an Ivy League school with an MBA in 1971, I toured Europe for twelve weeks with my roommate and then settled down as a freshman analyst with Interstate Securities (now Interstate/Johnson Lane) in Charlotte, North Carolina. Interstate had a small equity (stock) research department with a CPA, a nice fellow, as its director. One of the early lessons I learned at Interstate was never to make a CPA head of your research department. They may know their numbers, but they're usually not the greatest stock pickers.

Since I knew virtually nothing about stocks, the stock market, investing, or the economy, I was immediately assigned to review customer portfolios and make suggestions about what to buy and to sell. I'm glad our customers didn't know how little I knew. At the time, even I didn't realize how little I knew, but somehow I muddled through.

Three years into my career, the stock market entered a protracted bear market (bear markets fall, bull markets rise) that wouldn't finish killing investors until December

1974, two years after it began. This bear market was the most savage since the 1930s. It was my first but certainly not my last. The closing Dow Jones industrial average (the principal market index), which Dan Rather now reports every night on CBS, peaked in early 1973 at 1052 and finally troughed about twenty-four months later at 578, a 45 percent plunge.

Most of the stocks I and my department of analysts were recommending did far worse. Some fell 80 percent or more, and that was not particularly atypical. Brokerage houses across America were enduring similar fates. Besides all my recommendations being pounded beneath the floor, I lost about 75 percent of my personal portfolio in the carnage. After it was all over but while I was still thinking the world might end any day, I decided it was time to take a different track. By then I had been put in charge of the research efforts. Toward the end of 1975 I was officially named research director and an officer of the firm.

By this point, three important lessons were engraved in my cranium:

1. Don't let a CPA run your research department.
2. Make sure an analyst knows what he's doing before you turn him loose on your customers.
3. Bear markets hurt.

Armed with these invaluable bits of wisdom, I set out on a quest to discover (1) how to keep from losing money, and (2) how to make substantial profits investing in companies. I had just entered a three-year program to become a chartered financial analyst (CFA), which is the security-analyst equivalent of a CPA in accounting. The most important thing I learned in the CFA program was discovering a book called *Security Analysis* by Benjamin Graham and David Dodd. Though this book was no longer used in the program, I found out it was a book I needed to own, so I purchased it and began the slow slog through its six-hundred-plus pages.

I uncovered one concept Graham developed—margin of safety—and took it to heart. There's more about this in chapter 3, Valuable Lessons from Benjamin Graham. Warren Buffett, Graham's best and wealthiest student (he's worth more than $18 billion) at Columbia, likened margin of safety to building a bridge to accommodate forty tons, but nothing heavier than ten tons ever crosses it.

As Interstate's research director, I urged all the analysts to become students of Benjamin Graham and to adhere strictly to the margin-of-safety concept. In late 1974, contrary to the industry, we began keeping records of all our recommendations and how they stacked up against the market indexes. We also told our brokers and customers that when we thought it was time to sell a stock we'd say so in writing. Margin of safety worked. The research record, published annually, served as a check. When I left Interstate at the end of 1985, our research department had compiled an eleven-year performance record that was the envy of Wall Street.

Since I began my newsletter, *The Staton Institute*ˢᴹ *Advisory,* in January 1986, I have published my record frequently. Every stock recommended to my clients (from the time I say buy to when I say sell) gained an average 29.62 percent annualized, compared with 13.2 percent for the Standard & Poor's 500 index. That's a record few other money experts can touch.

Now that I've shown you my track record, you're going to learn why stocks have always been, and will continue to be, the most profitable investment. The historical evidence is overwhelming, so I'll show you only a little of it. From there, you'll learn the value of a simple investment program. We'll examine what it takes for a company to become one of America's Finest, and you'll get an up-close look at 4 of the 397 that constitute the AFC universe.

Although it's tempting to pay a professional to take charge of your money, in most cases I don't recommend it. You really can have superior results if you do it yourself. My daughter, who's nineteen now, started her own portfolio at age ten, and since then has beat more than two-thirds of the professional money managers. From May 1988 through July 31, 1997, the initial $4,300 investment has swelled to $23,000. If she can do it, you can, too!

Good old Uncle Sam and the state where you live will gladly help you make more money if you'd be interested in deferring taxes for years, if not decades, down the road Most people don't know how to take advantage of Uncle's generosity, but I'll teach you how to make it work for you.

Being your own money manager sounds like a lot of hard work, but really it isn't. Is sixty minutes too much time to spend each year? That's the time most Americans use for lunch each day. I'm only asking for about one hour annually. That's all it takes, and you can become a millionaire if you'll stick with this easy-to-start-and-maintain investment program. If you don't need the annual cash dividends from your stocks for personal use, I'll show you how to make them make more money. I'll even show you how to buy shares direct and bypass the stockbroker. You can save thousands of dollars over a lifetime of investing.

You have to open your investment account somewhere. The mechanics aren't difficult. I'll show you how to get started the easiest way.

Do you want to embark your children on an investment program as I did with my daughter in 1988? The earlier they start, the more successful they'll be. What about giving money and securities to your children? We'll look at that option, too. Then we'll move into the companies themselves. There are 397 listed in the appendix at the back of the book along with lots of helpful statistics. There's plenty of good merchandise from which to choose. There's something for everybody.

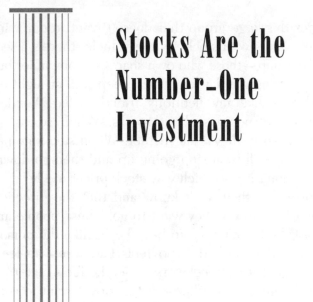

CHAPTER TWO

Stocks Are the Number-One Investment

It makes me nervous when I'm not nervous about the stock market.

—WILLIE WONDER

Millions of Americans are afraid to buy shares of companies. They get goose bumps just thinking about putting money into stocks, even of the top-rated companies, because they reason that one day prices might go over the cliff as they did between 1929 and 1932. Investing in stocks is as terrifying to them as skydiving would be to me. That's why I don't do it—skydiving that is.

Besides this large group that doesn't want to enter investment waters with stocks as the vehicle, there's a second large group—those who own shares of companies but are antsy during the day and don't sleep well at night either. They're like my fictitious friend Willie Wonder. They're always nervous about stocks. When stocks go down, they worry they'll fall further. When stocks go up, they worry they'll soon stop going up and then go down. Or if they don't know which way stock prices are headed, they worry that they don't know and that the direction might not be the way they want to go. These people are worrywarts and don't need to be. They're like the person George Burns described "who feels bad when he feels good for fear that he'll feel worse when he feels better."

If you fit into either of these categories, I want to convince you: Stocks are a great place to have your money, the safest, least risky place of all. Just for the moment, put aside any hesitation you may have and accept these words. You can always change your mind later. I believe that when you finish this chapter you'll know why stocks have always been, and will continue to be, the number-one investment. I don't want you to feel about investing in stocks as Gertrude Stein, the American writer, did about life in general, "There ain't any answer. There ain't going to be any answer. There never has been an answer. That's the answer."

Before we get into why stocks are right for almost everyone, I'll share a little history about how stocks came to be and why they *always* go up when given enough time.

By the time Columbus set sail for what he thought were the East Indies (he landed in the Caribbean instead), shares of various commodities and what were then called joint-stock companies were actively bought and sold in Antwerp, Belgium. The city of Antwerp claims that, of the world's 150-odd stock exchanges, its exchange is the oldest, having been found in 1531. Amsterdam lays claim to the second with a start-up date of 1602.

Stock certificates of ownership were sold to investors in some European countries to finance powerhouse enterprises like the United East India Company, which came to life in 1602. This phenomenal company returned about 18 percent annually to investors for three decades ($1 grew to more than $143), an incredible performance, and remained in business until 1799.

Stock trading on a limited basis existed well before Jesus was born. The early Romans formed joint-stock companies and sold pieces of them to the public. The word *company* is from *cum* (with) and *panis* (bread) because business, even in those days, was often conducted over a meal, as it so frequently is today. Under the law, joint-stock companies of that time could do just two things—government contracting and tax collecting. What fantastic businesses to invest in! Capital (money) was raised by selling *partes* (shares) to willing investors.

Securities markets in the United States can be traced to the late 1700s. In 1789, Congress authorized and issued $80 million of government bonds to pay down war debts and to inject money into this fledgling country's economy, thereby creating the first "money market." According to *American Heritage* magazine, "The new United States was desperately short of money in any reliable or secured form. Accounts were still kept in pounds, shillings, and pence."

Brokers (they were first called stockjobbers) traded

securities literally in the street. The word *broker* was derived from wine merchants, who broached (tapped) their wine kegs. *Broacher* was later shortened to *broker*. Brokers bought and sold primarily government bonds as well as any stocks offered by the infant Bank of the United States. When the weather turned sour, they retreated to coffeehouses (presumably to warm up) and carried on their business.

The several dozen established brokers operated a highly risky "market." James Madison was so concerned he fired off a letter to Thomas Jefferson warning that "stock jobbing drowns every other subject. The coffeehouse is an eternal buzz with the gamblers." Since stock brokering, trading, or whatever you want to call it was so risky in the early days, the phrase "gambling in the stock market" still has deep meaning for most Americans.

In 1792, twenty-four brokers and merchants gathered at Corre's Hotel to sign the Buttonwood Agreement, which was written front and back on a sheet of paper:

> We, the Subscribers, Brokers for the Purchase and Sale of Public Stocks, do hereby solemnly pledge ourselves to each other that we will not buy or sell, from this day, for any person whatsoever, any kind of Public Stock at a less rate than one-quarter per cent Commission on the Special value, and that we will give preference to each other in our negotiations.

This unusual contract laid the foundation for the later-to-be-formed (in 1817) New York Stock & Exchange Board. The following winter the brokers built a home for themselves, the Tontine Coffee House, on the corner of Water and Wall streets in New York, then the nation's capital.

The famous street named Wall, one of the best known in the world, is only four blocks long. It lies on the site of the original wall (stockade) built at the tip of Manhattan Island. In 1644, Dutch settlers laid a brushwood barrier to keep Indians out and cattle in. Nine years later Governor Peter Stuyvesant replaced it with a nine-foot-high palisade. Wall Street is named for this barrier, not for the high buildings on both sides of the street that currently create walls.

"Wall Street" is the common name for the American financial institutions, markets, and mechanisms that formalized and democratized the capital-formation (money-raising) process that helps companies thrive. Wall Street, with the New York Stock Exchange as its flagship, has allowed millions of Americans to participate in this country's unmatched growth through ownership of common stocks. *Life* magazine, in its spring 1992 issue, dedicated to the Big Board, observed, "For two centuries, men (and, much more recently, women) have met at the convergence of Wall and Broad streets in lower Manhattan to buy, sell and haggle, all in the name of capitalism. They have not always done so politely . . . or fairly. But as Americans traded, so the country was built. Canals, Railroads, Automobiles, Electronics. Ideas may spring from laboratories, but the money that turns them into reality is raised here."

With capitalism rapidly spreading across the globe, new stock exchanges have recently sprouted behind what used to be the Iron Curtain. Poland opened a stock market in early 1991 in the old Communist Party headquarters (ironic, isn't it?). The Polish market was funded by British money and modeled after France's Bourse, another name for stock exchange or place of meeting to conduct business. Initially, trading took place only once a week in five different companies, but the government expects lots more, since it plans to privatize more than 3,500 firms under its control. Communist Party headquarters must be luxurious because St. Petersburg opened its exchange (*The Wall Street Journal* calls a stock exchange the "icon of capitalism") on the third floor of its own party building.

What exactly is a common stock? It's a security (stock certificate) representing proportionate ownership (an investor's share) of a publicly traded company. There are more than sixteen thousand public companies in America. You can buy shares in most of them through any stockbroker. These shares are traded (bought and sold) on either the New York Stock Exchange (NYSE), the American Stock Exchange (ASE), or NASDAQ Over-the-Counter (OTC). They range in price from a penny to more than $38,000 for Berkshire-Hathaway on the NYSE.

Where did the word *stock* come from? Here's my theory. William Bradford, governor of the Plymouth Colony, reported that under an agreement with the Pilgrims' sponsors from England, "all profit" (crops, fish, and trade goods) would "remain still in the common stock." All Pilgrims were allowed to obtain their food and goods from the common stock (to share), just as all investors can make their profits by investing (sharing) in the "common stock" of public companies.

Stocks are priced in points instead of dollars. One point equals $1.00. One-half point equals $0.50, one-quarter point $0.25, one-eighth point $0.125. Stocks trade in eighths rather than tenths like money. Isn't that strange? There's a practical reason. When stock trading began in colonial days, coins were in short supply. To make coinage go further, Spanish silver dollars were sliced into halves, then halved and halved again. The result? The dollar could be divided into eight bits. Each bit was one eighth of a dollar. Together, eight bits became a "piece of eight."

Note: Since the first printing of this book in 1995, stocks on the New York Stock Exchange have begun trading in increments of one sixteenth, or 6.25 cents. Prices are to be quoted in decimals instead of fractions by January 2000.

Here's how stocks work. In this example, MakeMoney Enterprises (MME), a fictitious company, has 1 million shares outstanding. Each share sells for 20 (note: stock prices are quoted without the dollar sign), so MME's total stock is worth $20 million. If you invest $4,000 in MME at its current price, you can purchase two hundred shares.

When you purchase your shares, you will own part of the company. Although it's a tiny part (⅟₅₀₀₀), it's all yours. Now that you are part owner of MME, what good is it? Let's use this example to find out.

MME earns $2 million after taxes in 1998. Dividing earnings by the number of shares (1 million), each share has $2.00. MME provides money out of earnings, a cash dividend, as incentive for you to buy and hold its shares. (Not all companies pay dividends, but the bulk of America's Finest Companies do.) Out of the $2.00 per share of earnings, MME pays you half, $1.00. The dollar is your immediate reward for owning a piece of the company.

	1998	2003	2008
MME share price	20	??	??
MME earnings per share	$2.00	$3.00	$5.00
MME dividend per share	$1.00	$1.50	$2.50
MME keeps (retains)	$1.00	$1.50	$2.50

23

MME keeps (retains) the other half and plows it back into the business for reasons similar to humans eating daily to survive. Retained earnings go for research and product development, to build a new plant, to purchase new equipment, to hire more people—to grow.

By keeping the dollar not paid you, MME is now worth $1.00 more per share for each share outstanding than before. The company's total asset value increases $1 million (1 million shares times $1.00 per share retained). MME's business prospers. Five years from now its earnings have risen 50 percent to $3.00 per share. And as further reward to you for holding the shares as opposed to selling them, the company boosts its dividend (as it has done every year since you bought your shares) to the newest annual rate of $1.50. Each year it keeps as much as it pays you, and that amount kept annually enhances MME's value.

Your annual income is increasing. By 2008, earnings per share are $5.00. Your dividend is now $2.50 per share, up 150 percent over 1998. The company keeps $2.50 per share that year, $2.5 million total, to further boost asset value by that amount.

QUESTION: If the share price is 20 in 1998 when you buy into MME, and the shares are not overpriced, do you think the price will be higher in 2003 than in 1998? Will it be even higher in 2008?

ANSWER: If the share price maintains the same relationship to its earnings and dividend, it will rise to 30 in 2003 and to 50 by 2008.

Your original investment of two hundred shares at 20 each will be worth $10,000 in 2008. Your cost: $4,000.

Your profit: $6,000. Between 1998 and 2008, your annual income from MME will jump from $200 to $500. Your yield on original investment will rise to 12.5 percent ($500 divided by $4,000), a handsome return.

Over a period of years, the majority of publicly owned companies grow. (All the companies in the AFC universe are growing; otherwise they wouldn't be included.) Growing companies earn more money. They pay out more cash as dividends. They plow back a growing stream of earnings into their businesses, thus enhancing the value of those businesses. This explains why stock prices *always* go up in the long run. The Dow Jones industrial average, the most famous measure of stock prices, rose from 88 in 1912 to more than 8000 by the end of July 1997. That's from price appreciation alone and excludes cash dividends.

You need to know a little background about the Dow Jones average because it is by far the most widely followed stock-market index in the world. Coming out of what is sometimes known as "the other great depression," the depression of 1893, stocks were for gamblers. Prudent, conservative investors purchased only bonds.

Charles H. Dow (along with partner Edward D. Jones and a fellow named Bergstrasser) wanted a gauge, a thermometer for the growth of America, so the Dow industrial average was born. Whereas there are more than eighteen hundred companies of all sorts listed on the New York Stock Exchange today, then about 60 percent were railroads. Most companies' stocks were illiquid, meaning they couldn't be readily bought or sold without markedly disturbing the price.

The Dow was first published on May 26, 1896, with a dozen industrial companies and a beginning level of 40.94.

It has since soared as high as 8100 and changed considerably. General Electric (originally Edison General Electric Company) is the sole survivor from the original Dow among the thirty current companies.

Some time ago, H. Bradlee Perry, chairman of the David L. Babson investment counseling firm, neatly summed up investing in stocks this way: "In the long run the price of just about every individual stock and the market value of all stocks together are determined by the growth of earnings and dividends. This is so simple that many of the sophisticated people in our [investing] field seem to overlook it. That is too bad because it does provide the basis for a very sound and unworrisome investment approach.

"Over the span of many decades corporate profits and dividends have trended upward in all industrial nations because their economies have expanded, not without business cycle interruptions of course, but in an inexorable trend of long-term growth."

You can participate in America's future growth by owning shares of common stock in a variety of businesses. But by investing in companies in America's Finest Companies, you're assured their businesses will continue to thrive and increase in value. As they do, so will the value of the stocks themselves and the cash dividends they pay. This is the reason you want to own your part of corporate America with America's Finest Companies. Stocks have outperformed all other investments for two hundred years.

The great patriot Patrick Henry addressed the Virginia Convention in 1775: "I know of no way of judging of the future but by the past." The past is important to investors because it gives us a picture of the future returns we can

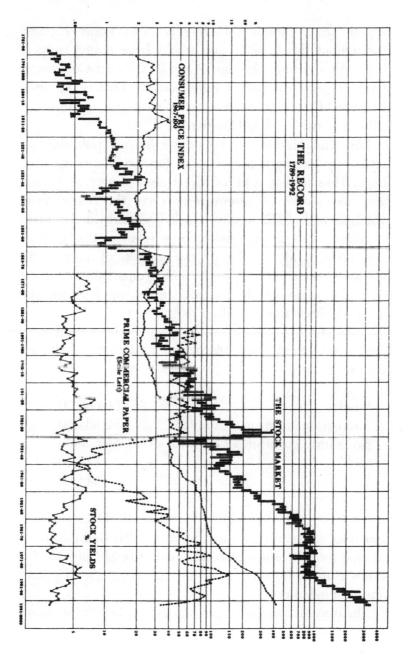

expect from various investments. The point I stress throughout this book is that stocks have always outperformed everything else, and America's Finest Companies have outperformed most other stocks. That being true, why would you want to invest your money in anything besides America's Finest Companies?

The scholarly *Financial Analysts Journal* published an article by Jeremy J. Siegel in its January–February 1992 issue. He's studied a lot of investment history, as I have, and here's what he discovered: "Over the period from 1802 through 1992, equity [stocks] has provided returns superior to those on fixed-income investments, gold or commodities. Most strikingly, the real rate of return [with inflation taken out] on equity held remarkably constant over this period while the real return on fixed-income assets declined dramatically."

Going back to 1802, this is what $1.00 would have grown to by the end of 1992 without taking taxes into account.

Stocks	$3,050,000.00
Short-term government bonds	$2,934.00
Long-term government bonds	$6,620.00
Gold	$13.40
Inflation	$11.80

Over 190 years, stocks grew to be worth 1,040 times as much as short-term government bonds, 461 times as much as long-term government bonds, and astonishingly 227,612 times as much as gold. Stocks also came out 258,475 times ahead of inflation.

The obvious conclusion is—stocks knocked the socks off

bonds and other fixed-income investments like savings accounts, money-market funds, and certificates of deposit. Since 1926 (the first year of Standard & Poor's stock-price index), the compound annual return of all stocks listed on the NYSE, after subtracting inflation, was 6.4 percent compared with only 0.5 percent for Treasury bills. To say it another way, money invested in T-bills or ordinary savings accounts would have taken 139 years to double compared to only 11 years in stocks. America's Finest Companies work even faster.

Speaking of inflation, over every thirty-year period from 1802 through 1996, there were only two when the annual total return from stocks wasn't at least 3.5 percentage points ahead of the consumer price index. They occurred in the Great Depression. Highest real (after inflation is deducted) returns were in the 1960s and outdistanced inflation by more than 10 percentage points.

At this point, I bet I know what you're thinking: Everybody knows how well real estate has done. That's where all the great fortunes are made. Wrong! I'm going to talk about real estate and pop one of the great investing bubbles. Despite what you think or have heard or read, real estate is not as good as stocks.

The Harris Bank of Chicago analyzed returns from seven assets over three periods of time covering nearly one hundred years. I converted their data into the table on page 31 and updated it through 1985. Stocks were the hands-down winner all three times.

Stocks, after inflation was removed, earned a 6.0 to 6.9 percent compound annual return, far ahead of any of the other investments including farmland and housing.

Will stocks do as well in the future as they have in the

past? Will they remain the number-one investment? History resoundingly says the answer is "Yes." Every long-term study I've ever seen says that, given enough time, stocks will be the best investment.

Since stocks offer the best return on investment compared to anything else, why are certificates of deposit and money-market funds so popular today, especially in tax-deferred retirement plans? I think the answer must be because the principal is considered "safe." With a CD, people know exactly what their rate of return is going to be. A money-market fund doesn't earn a guaranteed rate, but it is easy to get into and out of, and the return can be closely estimated in three- and six-month periods. Unfortunately, the vast majority of people mistakenly perceive that returns from stocks are wildly uncertain. That is not true except over very short periods of time.

George F. Baker, founder of First National Bank of New York (the forerunner of Citicorp), said that patience is one of three prerequisites for making a fortune in stocks. He knew time is on the side of the investor. He also knew that the longer you invest the better your results will be. History proves it. The table on page 31 spans seven decades.

History is the only guide investors have for the future. History shows that CD and money-market investments barely keep ahead of inflation. Their future rate of return, after taking out inflation, will likely approximate the historic returns from commercial paper and bonds shown in the table on page 31, about 1.5 percent per year. At that rate it will take forty-seven years for money to double. But if an investor's money is in a balanced stock portfolio, it will grow at 6 to 7 percent per year (after inflation) and

REAL RETURNS ON INVESTMENT ASSETS
(ANNUAL RETURNS WITH INFLATION REMOVED)

	HOUSING	FARMLAND	GOLD	SILVER	COMMERCIAL PAPER	BONDS	STOCKS
1890–1985	4.8%	N.A.	(0.3)%	1.9%	1.8%	1.5%	6.2%
1912–1985	4.7	4.5%	(0.5)	0.1	1.1	1.0	6.0
1950–1985	4.6	6.5	2.2	1.9	1.7	(0.2)	6.9

double in eleven to twelve years, four times as fast. In America's Finest Companies it will double even faster. I'll talk about how fast in chapter 7.

Like commercial paper and bonds, gold and silver have been and should continue to be poor places for money. Housing and farmland ought to generate nice returns in the future as they have in the past but not nearly as great as the returns from common stocks.

No one knows what the future return from common stocks will be, or the inflation rate. If I were to guess, and I will, I'd say stocks—over the next thirty, forty, fifty, or sixty years—will grow at 10 to 12 percent annually, with inflation in the 3–4 percent range. Why is this important to know? Because if stocks and inflation continue to increase at their historic rates, you can project what a given amount of money today will be worth (with inflation taken out) in the future. You can also see what the miracle of compound interest does when you invest in companies in America's Finest Companies.

Compounding can be traced back to the Babylonians. They were the original mathematicians, scientists, engineers, and financiers. Babylon is perhaps most famous for its hanging gardens. It was protected by a huge wall completely surrounding the city. Thousands of Babylonian writings on clay tablets have been discovered. Tables of compound growth, a law as secure as gravity, were among them.

Einstein considered compound interest to be humanity's greatest invention, since it allows for the systematic, reliable increase of wealth. Baron de Rothschild, when asked to name the seven wonders of the world, remarked,

BUY SHARES IN AMERICA'S FINEST COMPANIES AND HOLD THEM.
THE LONGER, THE BETTER.
(1926–1996)

	1 YEAR	5 YEARS	10 YEARS	20 YEARS
Holding periods (years from 1926)	71	67	62	52
Times outpacing inflat on	48 (68%)	53 (79%)	55 (89%)	52 (100%)
Times with positive returns	51 (72%)	60 (90%)	60 (97%)	52 (100%)
Times with negative returns	20 (28%)	7 (10%)	2	0

Copyright © 1997 The Staton Institute℠, Inc.

"I cannot. But I know that the eighth wonder is compound interest."

Sidney Homer, formerly with the investment-banking firm of Salomon Brothers, described the awesome benefits of compound interest this way: "One thousand dollars left to earn interest at 8 percent a year will be worth twenty-three quadrillion dollars [$23,000,000,000,000,000] in four hundred years, but the first hundred years are the hardest."

CHAPTER THREE

Valuable Lessons from Benjamin Graham

To achieve satisfactory investment results is easier than most people realize.

The typical individual investor has a great advantage over the large institutions.

      —BENJAMIN GRAHAM

As stock prices fell relentlessly, day after day, week after week (I was so depressed it often seemed second after second) in the savage bear market of 1973–74, I was beginning to think I'd entered the wrong profession. What good was it being a Wharton-trained securities analyst when all my stock recommendations were getting clobbered?

When the Great Bear finally went into hibernation in fall 1974, I'd been in the securities profession exactly three years and three months. By that time, I'd been named "coordinator" of my firm's research efforts. I thought "coordinator" was a strange title, but it was better than nothing and at least it meant I was in charge. Shortly after being appointed to that role, I was made an officer and research director.

Between January 1973 and December 1974, the Dow Jones industrial average, the most popular stock-price index, plunged 45 percent. Only two other drops since World War I had been worse. One was during the Great Depression. The Dow reached 381 in 1929. By the end of 1932 it had gotten as low as 41, an 89 percent fall, nearly twice as deep as 1973–74. The other was 1937–38, when the Dow declined 49 percent in a mini-depression.

The few stock recommendations I'd made up to that time had collapsed in value, along with everything else my fellow analysts had on the buy list. Looking back at the carnage was as painful to me as it must have been to all the South Floridians who saw what Hurricane Andrew did to where they used to live. My personal portfolio shed nearly 75 percent of its value, and I kept wondering how many millions, if not hundreds of millions, of dollars my company's customers had lost.

I tend to bounce back quickly, so rather than dwell on what had gone wrong, as research chief I began to search for a method, any method, that would prevent the devastating losses of 1973–74 from ever afflicting me or any of my clients in the future. I was working on my Chartered

Financial Analyst certification, which would take other analysts three years to complete. Not me. I used four because I really enjoyed giving up a beautiful Saturday each June to endure a six-hour marathon exam.

I discovered that some years earlier the CFA program had used a different book from the one I'd been studying; it was *Security Analysis,* by Benjamin Graham and David Dodd. A third author, Sydney Cottle, was a later contributor. This bible of security analysts was originally published in 1934 shortly after the worst stock collapse in U.S. history ended.

The third edition, which I own, was essentially a rewriting rather than a revision of the original. When it came out in 1951, Benjamin Graham was president of the Graham-Newman Corporation, a money-management operation, and guest professor at Columbia University's graduate school of business. His collaborator and colleague, David L. Dodd, was a professor of finance there. What struck me about this particular edition was that it was dedicated to what the authors termed the "New Generation of Security Analysts." I'll never be able to ask either Graham or Dodd what they meant, but I suppose they were thinking World War II had escorted in a new era, both for the economy and for analyzing stocks and other securities. Their revised version was meant to educate a new breed of analysts and get them off on the proper footing.

Benjamin Graham is called the principal author of the five editions of *Security Analysis.* When he died in Aix-en-Provence in 1976 at age eighty-two, he was a millionaire. The dean of security analysts had sold more than 100,000 copies of his book before his passing. That's quite a large total for any book, especially a textbook.

Graham, born in 1894, grew up in New York, where he received his bachelor of science degree from Columbia in 1914. On graduating Phi Beta Kappa, Graham went to work on Wall Street. His first job was chalking up stock and bond prices on a board. From that lowly position he became a runner who delivered securities and checks, then on to assistant of a two-man bond department, where he wrote concise descriptions of the bonds in inventory to be sold. He also began writing a daily market letter.

Ben Graham was so proficient and got along so well with people he soon became a customers' man and personally visited customers as a bond salesman. A salesman he wasn't but a quick study he was. Young Graham soon realized how little his firm's customers really knew about the bonds they were buying and selling. He was later named a partner in the Wall Street firm of Newburger, Henderson & Loeb.

During the roaring bull market of the 1920s, Graham and Jerome Newman formed the Graham-Newman Corporation and an investment partnership, Newman & Graham. Even though they were pummeled in the 1929–32 stock freefall, their partnership churned out impressive returns (17.4 percent annually) before they dissolved it in 1956. Ten thousand dollars invested in Graham-Newman in 1936 threw off about $2,100 per year in income for the next twenty years (roughly $42,000), and the original principal was repaid when it liquidated.

I've often joked that *Security Analysis* isn't called the "bible of the trade" for nothing. It's thick, it's not easy or fun reading, and far too many of the professionals who have read it ignore many of its basic principles, just as have most readers of the Bible, the world's best-selling book.

The edition I studied was the fourth, which had further refinements over the previous three, but the guts of it were still the same. I bought a copy and began to trudge through it on my own time. "Trudge" is the right word because, as in medical textbooks, there was much to learn on each page. I absorbed many lessons from Benjamin Graham, including his famous margin-of-safety concept: buy when stock prices overall are undervalued or pick out specific issues with promising prospects that sell well below their intrinsic worth.

When Graham started on Wall Street, a formal method for establishing the true value of stocks and bonds was all but nonexistent. There were various theories about how to speculate successfully in stocks, but not much attention was paid to investing. Speculating was a game of sorts. Graham knew investing to be the opposite, that it could and should be scientific. He believed basic principles could be uncovered that would enable students of the trade to learn how to buy $1.00 of assets at far less than their true worth. If this could be done, he reasoned, it was possible to earn handsome profits because few, if any, others were approaching securities analysis from such a solid quantitative base.

Since he was a teacher by nature and profession, Graham wanted to make his scientific investing principles available to others. That strong desire led him to write the epic on how to analyze securities. Unfortunately, *Security Analysis* is so unwieldy it has never reached the masses of individual investors as Graham so fervently desired, and it has managed to bypass more than its fair share of Wall Street's best. Although the tools for investment success are within its pages, Graham's techniques are so cumbersome the vast majority of people whom he wanted to benefit, even if they were interested, didn't have the time to, and could never, put them to work.

Even so, Benjamin Graham's works and his various interviews and research papers were tremendously interesting to me. I was absorbed by everything I could learn from and about this investment master. I was especially fascinated to discover that Graham's primary reason for continually perfecting his craft was to show how to invest safely and with as little effort as possible.

This passion to share the gospel of investing with anyone who would listen led him to write *The Intelligent Investor* in 1949. In the introduction of a later edition of the book, Graham made certain the reader knew he wasn't writing for those who liked high risk or spending lots of time on their portfolios. Right away he had my attention.

Instead, *The Intelligent Investor* was dedicated to the defensive or passive investor who wanted to avoid large losses and the hassle of worrying about his investment strategy. Graham observed that the investor's worst enemy is himself or herself: "We have seen much more money made and *kept* by 'ordinary people' who were temperamentally well suited for the investment process than by those who lacked this quality, even though they had an extensive knowledge of finance, accounting, and stock-market lore." He made another astute observation: "Sound investment principles produced generally sound results."

By the time Graham was in his eighties, still as sharp as ever, financial institutions—brokerage firms, banks, insurance companies, and the like—were spending millions of dollars a year and grinding out thousands of pages of research on this or that security. This was the opposite of what was occurring when Ben Graham had stepped onto Wall Street some fifty years earlier. Little time or effort was then exerted on practical securities research. The kind of in-depth analysis Graham pioneered paid off handsomely, since there was virtually no competition.

As he grew older, Graham realized hordes of others were attempting to follow in his giant footsteps, so many in fact that they were bumping into one another while trying to pick undervalued securities—especially stocks— that would rise in value. He thought that since Wall Street was pouring such vast resources into stock research, the elaborate techniques he devised were rapidly losing their value. It seemed to be a case of what everybody else knows isn't worth knowing.

Graham communicated this view shortly before his death in 1976 in his final interview, which appeared in the September-October 1976 *Financial Analysts Journal*. Only one person in the United States is customarily introduced with no introduction—the President. Benjamin Graham was introduced almost as reverently as one "who needs no introduction to the readers of this magazine." Excerpts from that last interview appear here.

In the light of your sixty-odd years of experience in Wall Street, what is your overall view of common stocks?

Common stocks have one important investment characteristic and one important speculative characteristic. Their investment value and average market price tend to increase irregularly but persistently over the decades, as their net worth builds up through the reinvestment of undistributed earnings. However, most of the time common stocks are subject to irrational and excessive price fluctuations in both directions, as the consequence of the ingrained tendency of most people to speculate or gamble—i.e., to give way to hope, fear and greed.

What is your view of the financial community as a whole?

Most of the stockbrokers, financial analysts, investment advisers, etc., are above average in intelligence, business honesty and sincerity. But they lack adequate experience with all types of security markets and an overall understanding of common stocks—of what I call "the nature of the beast." They tend to take the market and themselves too seriously. They spend a large part of their time trying, valiantly and ineffectively, to do things they can't do well.

What sort of things, for example?

To forecast short- or long-term changes in the economy, and in the price level of common stocks, to select the most promising industry groups and individual issues—generally for the near-term future.

Can the average manager of institutional funds obtain better results than the Dow Jones Industrial Average or the Standard & Poor's Index over the years?

No. In effect, that would mean that the stock market experts as a whole could best themselves—a logical contradiction.

Turning now to individual investors, do you think that they are at a disadvantage compared with the institutions, because of the latter's huge resources, superior facilities for obtaining information, etc.?

On the contrary, the typical individual investor has a great advantage over the large institutions.

What general rules would you offer the individual investor for his investment policy over the years?

Let me suggest three such rules: (1) The individual investor should act consistently as an investor and not as a speculator. (2) The investor should have a definite selling policy for all his common stock commitments, corresponding to his buying techniques. (3) Finally, the investor should always have a minimum percentage of his total portfolio in common stocks and a minimum percentage in bond equivalents.

In selecting the common stock portfolio, do you advise careful study of and selectivity among individual issues?

In general, no. I am no longer an advocate of elaborate techniques of security analysis in order to find superior value opportunities. This was a rewarding activity, say, forty years ago, when our textbook "Graham and Dodd" was first published; but the situation has changed a good deal since then. In the old days any well-trained security analyst could do a good professional job of selecting undervalued issues through detailed studies; but in the light of the enormous amount of research now being carried on, I doubt whether in most cases such extensive efforts will generate sufficiently superior selections to justify their cost.

In addressing the question about how individuals should create and manage their common-stock portfolios, Graham gave the two specific methods he preferred, both of which require a good deal of work on the part of the individual. He followed by saying that "to enjoy a reasonable chance for continued better-than-average results, the investor must follow policies which are (1) inherently sound and promising, and (2) are not popular in Wall Street," and "Investment is most intelligent when it is most businesslike."

In addition to margin-of-safety, the cornerstone of the Benjamin Graham philosophy of investing, these are the other valuable lessons I learned from him:

1. Stock prices rise "irregularly but persistently" over time because the value of the underlying businesses continues to increase as retained earnings are plowed back into those businesses.
2. Financial professionals, on the whole, are well educated, honest, and sincere but have a shallow understanding of common stocks.
3. Professionals spend far too much time trying to do what can't be done—predicting the future of the economy, the level of stock prices, and which industries and individual stocks will perform best.
4. The average professional money manager cannot beat the market as measured by the Dow Jones industrials, Standard & Poor's 500, or some other principal index. Professionals are the average, and it's a "logical contradiction" that they can "best themselves."
5. Individuals have tremendous advantages over the professionals.
6. In order to be most successful, individual investors (a) must invest rather than speculate, (b) have a rule of thumb for the appropriate time to sell, and (c) always have at least a minimum of their portfolios in stocks.

7. Complicated techniques of security analysis aren't necessary to unearth superior opportunities.

8. The stock-picking method an investor uses should be rational and easy to apply and have "an excellent supporting record." Investment that is most "businesslike" will generate the best returns, especially when it goes against the grain of Wall Street.

By investing in America's Finest Companies the way I'll detail, you'll be aligning yourself with the investment wisdom and success of Benjamin Graham, the father of security analysis and a multimillionaire when he died. I can't say for certain whether Ben Graham would endorse my techniques, but I strongly believe he would. They meet all the criteria outlined in his farewell interview. They are time-proven and they work. What else could an investor want?

CHAPTER FOUR

Investing with America's Finest Companies Is the Simplest Way to Make Above-Average Profits

The simpler your investment plan, the more likely it will work.

—U.S. NEWS & WORLD REPORT

A simple investment program—one that is uncomplicated, readily understood, and easily implemented—is best because it's efficient. Simple investing will work very well for you, as it does for me and other knowledgeable investors. Garfield Drew, a noted stock-market technician (one who charts market and individual stock patterns as a guide to the future) of the 1950s, stated, "Simplicity or singleness of approach is a greatly underestimated factor of market success."

When people think of investing, simplicity is the last thing they think of. Everyone knows that investing (setting aside money today for the future) is a complex chore and not any fun either, right? Fun is not mentioned in investment books, courses in securities analysis, or investment letters (except mine). It should be. Having fun while you invest is critical to success. My strong belief is that if investing in stocks isn't fun for you, it won't be nearly as profitable as it can be.

Even if investing is profitable but you're not having fun (you constantly worry about day-to-day fluctuations in stock prices, or what you heard on *Wall Street Week*, or what the Federal Reserve did with the money supply, or the direction of the economy, or which way inflation and interest rates will go, or that the fifteen newsletters you subscribe to render conflicting advice, or ABC News says we're on the brink of recession, or some of the above or all of the above), you should try a new strategy.

The one I'm unfurling here is a good one. It's simple. It's rational. It produces superior results. It's fun. And it will beat most professional money managers year in and year out. My method is too simple for Wall Street to adopt, so they ignore it.

Benjamin Graham was asked in 1976 whether he recommended "careful study of and selectivity among individual issues." He responded, "In general, no. I am no longer an advocate of elaborate techniques of security analysis in order to find superior value opportunities."

My own studies dating back to the early 1920s confirm exactly what Graham said. The more complicated your stock-market strategy, the more difficult it is to implement and to monitor. What's worse, it almost always leads to mediocre performance. Simple is far better. The pros make investing complicated, but it doesn't have to be.

If you think about it for fifteen seconds, you readily see why investment counselors, financial advisors, stockbrokers, and money managers at banks, insurance companies, and mutual funds rarely beat the market indexes. Even those professionals who try to duplicate the market's results almost always fail. Here's why:

The Dow Jones industrials and Standard & Poor's 500 have no operating expenses. They go up and down without transaction costs. The money manager, trying to make his portfolio match one or the other market index, has to make frequent buys and sells to keep his portfolio in proportion with the stocks that make up the index he's working so hard to match. Stocks cost money to buy. They cost money to sell. The costs of trading, by themselves, make attempts to equal a market index virtually impossible.

If he's trying to beat the market instead of just equal it, the money manager has another dilemma. He usually cannot adopt a fun, businesslike, simple approach to investing like the one within these pages. Why? Because he (or she) wouldn't have to work a forty-hour week. He'd be taking so much time off, yet beating the indexes consistently, his boss would fire him. How could a company justify paying a money manager a full year's salary when he didn't have to work every day to profitably execute his investment plan?

The prudent money manager—one who wishes to remain employed—must create activities to fill his time. These include reading voluminous industry and company reports, dining with the managements of companies he owns or might like to own, attending numerous presentations to security analysts and portfolio managers, talking with friends in the business, sitting through an untold number of investment-committee meetings, scanning in-depth and ultra-thick computer runs, plus listening to the latest Wall Street gossip.

By doing all these things and more, the typical money manager's day is out of his control. He drowns in wasteful short-term activities, which history shows don't produce above-average results. Yet he generally cannot quit because he can't afford to lose his salary. If you were in his shoes, would you be any different?

Fortunately, you don't have to get sucked into the rut of the typical money manager. You can go your own profitable way. And you'll start by buying only the shares of highest-quality companies, America's Finest. You won't learn that in other investment books. They dwell on this method or that for picking the next Wal-Mart, Home Depot, or other company that is sure to make a million dollars for you from a small amount of money. The reason these books generally aren't worth much, besides being hard to understand, is they focus on the wrong things. Choosing the "right" stocks for your portfolio is less important than any other step for stock-market success.

Of course you do have to pick companies for your portfolio. There are two characteristics to look for when you invest in shares of companies:

1. The companies are in sound financial condition and won't go out of business.
2. Earnings and dividends will continue to grow.

Where are these companies? You can go out and uncover them on your own. That's the harder way, but it can be interesting to do the research. Or you can do it the easier way and pick from the alphabetical list in the appendix.

If you'll turn to the list for just a moment and skim quickly through it, you'll see there are a lot of companies that are household words. One is Coca-Cola, perhaps the most famous name in the world.

Fifteen of the thirty Dow industrials are included in America's Finest Companies. Coca-Cola is one. Another is Procter & Gamble, one of the world's premier consumer-products companies. Merck is a major pharmaceutical firm, while McDonald's sells more hamburgers (and owns more commercial real estate) than any other company in America. The others are DuPont, Exxon, General Electric, Minnesota Mining & Manufacturing, J. P. Morgan, Philip Morris, Walt Disney, Wal-Mart Stores, Johnson & Johnson, Hewlett-Packard, and Travelers Group.

When you invest your money, you want it to be 100 percent safe. Will Rogers used to say, "Forget about a return ON my investment. What I want is a return OF my investment." When you buy shares of companies in America's Finest Companies, you are 99.9 percent guaranteed they'll remain in business. By investing in them exclusively, you know they will stay afloat in the worst economic storms.

Benjamin Graham believed in buying quality. In *The Intelligent Investor* he noted, "The risk of paying too high a price for good-quality stocks—while a real one—is not the chief hazard confronting the average buyer of securities. Observations over many years has taught us that the chief losses to investors come from the purchase of low-quality securities at times of favorable business conditions."

There are dozens and dozens of U.S. companies that have been around for well over a hundred years. Quite a few are among the corporations in America's Finest Companies. They've survived panics, financial crises, depressions, earthquakes, droughts, floods, political scandals, wars, and any other disaster you can name. Among these are "blue-chip" companies such as Colgate-Palmolive, J. P. Morgan, and Exxon. They've been through just about everything, yet are still healthy and growing.

"Blue chip" describes highly regarded enterprises that generally make up the Dow Jones industrial average and a large part of the S & P 500. Blue chips have long earnings and dividend histories and are assumed to be able to withstand the most adverse economic circumstances.

Not all the companies included in America's Finest Companies are blue chips by the widely accepted definition, but they are all highly regarded and have exceptional records—at least ten consecutive years of higher earnings and/or dividends per share. As a group, they are well above average in financial strength. They are the thoroughbreds of corporate America and should be on the shopping list for assembling your personal market-beating portfolio.

America's Finest Companies comprises the top 3 percent (397) of all U.S. public companies. How have they been able to string together at least ten years in a row of higher earnings or dividends per share when the other 97 percent of public companies have not? Have a lot of them gotten into industries that are so good it would be hard not to be superachievers, or have most of them just been lucky? Or are there other factors? Is it possible to find some common threads that tie this elite group of companies together?

In the next few pages, you'll learn about three of the companies in America's Finest Companies, each of which is in a different industry. You may be unfamiliar with all of them, or perhaps you've heard of at least one.

DUKE ENERGY CORP.

In 1994 a reporter from *Money* magazine called. She was compiling a story on all the companies whose stocks had garnered a positive total return (price appreciation plus dividends reinvested) every year from 1980 through the end of 1993. Using Standard & Poor's enormous database, this writer had identified only fifteen companies, and she wanted to know what they had in common. I quickly answered, "That's easy." She stammered, "But you don't even know the names of the companies."

"I don't need to know them," was my response. "I already know what they share in common. They're all in America's Finest Companies and have at least ten straight years of higher dividends per share." She then read the list of fifteen, and I was on the money. Thirteen of the fifteen were U.S. companies, and all were among *America's Finest.* The other two were foreign. Duke Power, as it was then called, was one of the select thirteen.

Duke was founded in 1904 by tobacco magnate James Buchanan Duke (who also gave birth to internationally renowned Duke University), initially to serve a growing regional textile industry. It is one of the nation's largest (and most efficient) investor-owned electric utilities, serving nearly 2 million customers in the central portion of North Carolina and the western part of South Carolina, an area we locals know as the Piedmont Carolinas. The company operates three nuclear-generating and eight coal-fired stations, as well as hydroelectric and combustion-turbine stations. Through its Associated Enterprises Group, Duke has a number of other, smaller, diversified operations that are growing faster than the company's basic energy business.

More than 60 percent of Duke's electricity is from nuclear power, which makes the company the second largest nuclear system in the United States. Duke's goal is that its Nuclear Generation Department "be in the top ten, not just in terms of safety, reliability, or electric rates, but also in terms of the cost of producing electricity." At the end of 1995, Duke's McGuire plant ranked eighth as measured by nonfuel operations and maintenance costs. Its Oconee plant was in eleventh place, followed by Catawba at twentieth. Interestingly, Duke's Oconee Nuclear Station is the only one in the world using a hydro station as a source of emergency power.

On November 25, 1996, Duke Power announced its intent to acquire PanEnergy Corp. of Houston, one of the nation's leading energy-services companies, with nearly forty thousand miles of natural-gas pipeline and deliveries that account for 15 percent of the natural gas consumed in the United States. PanEnergy is the country's fourth largest producer of natural-gas liquids, the third largest marketer of natural gas in Canada and the United States, and a leading marketer of electricity, liquefied petroleum gases, and related energy services.

The new company has a total market value exceeding

$23 billion. Duke believes it was a strategic merger "about growth, opportunity, and creating value. Companies that are positioned to help their customers find business solutions that optimize a broad array of energy products and services at competitive prices will be rewarded with satisfied shareholders, customers, and employees."

Most shareholders never read the prospectus when two companies merge. They simply throw it away or recycle it. But the ten-ounce tome (full of the usual fine print and exhibits) issued by Duke on March 13, 1997, was revealing. Page 5 noted that the merger would make the combined company "the premier provider of energy products and services in North America" and that it offered "significant opportunities for revenue enhancement and strategic financial benefits . . . to shareholders . . . as well as customers and employees." Other significant benefits included the ability to offer a full range of energy products and services, a stronger asset base, great diversification, and expanded management resources.

The Value Line Investment Survey (available through virtually any library) gives Duke Energy an A+ financial-strength rating, stock-price stability of 100 (the highest figure), 75 for price-growth persistence, and 85 for earnings predictability. A company can't score much higher than that regardless of its industry.

EMERSON ELECTRIC CORP.

Only twenty-four American companies (out of more than sixteen thousand trading publicly) have a combined total of at least fifty years of higher earnings and dividends per share and qualify to be on my ultra-exclusive "Super 50 Team." American Home Products occupies the number-one slot, with forty-four years of dividends and forty-five of earnings. AHP is closely tailed by Bank of Granite, with forty-three and forty-three respectively, while Emerson Electric is in the third slot, with forty straight years of higher dividends per share and thirty-nine of earnings.

To say that being on the Super 50 Team is a difficult achievement is an understatement. It's almost impossible to get on, and once a company makes the team it's even harder to stay on. Every year two or three drop off the list.

Emerson's CEO Charles (Chuck) Knight was featured on the cover of and profiled in the August 1, 1994, issue of *Forbes*. The magazine noted, "You don't really know what the term 'competitive' means until you spend some time with Knight." What does 107-year-old Emerson do? The easiest way to answer that is naming some of the brands the company owns: Skil, Dremel, and Craftsman power tools; In-Sink-Erator waste disposals; Copeland compressors; Rosemount instruments; and Browning, Sealmaster, and U.S. Electric motors in the power-transmission area. Definitely not the high-tech stuff the Microsofts of the world churn out. *Fortune* describes the company's businesses as "largely glamourless" and "competing in mostly mundane, mature markets."

Emerson operates nimbly in many highly competitive markets and for more than a decade has held price increases well below the inflation rate. Even so, the company's operating and net profit margins have gone up. The net margin is up 1.5 percent just since 1987. That's because Knight early on recognized the need to cut costs and restructure. He was far ahead of most of his competitors in doing so when he launched Emerson's "best-cost producer strategy," which has paid off handsomely.

Emerson is well known for its "exceptionally detailed" planning, which has been the subject of numerous college and graduate-school case studies. At the core is seeking to pinpoint problems before they occur, but if they do to jump on them and solve them immediately. After many years of cost-cutting its way to higher profits and seeing revenue stagnate, Knight, in the company's intensive multiday planning conferences, led the charge away from efficiency-is-everything thinking to growing the top line. Emerson also gravitated to longer-term, higher-risk growth with bigger payoffs rather than always fretting about short-term earnings.

In 1994, Knight began inciting his managers to raise revenue growth to 10 percent a year from under 5 percent at that time. *Fortune* noted that Knight "unleashed creativity" through "radically changing" the company's culture. Emerson's annual report highlights five key management initiatives: repositioning for growth, technology leadership and new products, global expansion, strategic partnerships, and best-cost producer. Other noteworthy accomplishments include net earnings exceeding $1 billion for the first time; success in fast-growing markets, including the Asia-Pacific region (a 20 percent sales gain); and more than 30 percent of sales from new products introduced in the past five years, another first.

As a testament to its outstanding future, Emerson announced in November 1996 that it would repurchase nearly 9 percent of all stock outstanding "over the next four to five years."

MEDTRONIC CORP.

On a chilly raw Sunday in February 1992, I was expecting about two hundred friends of my father, Harold, to come to a little hamlet in eastern North Carolina called Bethel to help celebrate his eightieth birthday. People who know Bethel know it has just one major intersection where U.S. highways 13 and coast-to-coast 64 cross. The local Da-Nite restaurant (owned and run by my college roommate) has always been a stopover point for travelers heading east toward Nags Head and the Outer Banks.

It was just past noon that day. My two children, my brother, his wife and their four children, and my girlfriend (now wife and business partner) Mary and her two kids were all gathered in my aunt Camille's kitchen for a wonderful buffet lunch. Suddenly my thirteen-year-old daughter, Gracie, collapsed. She lay writhing on the floor, passed out, and was rapidly turning blue. I knew it must be her heart because she had an arrhythmia, but none of us knew then that it could be lethal.

Gracie was experiencing sudden-cardiac death from ventricular fibrillation, a condition in which the two bottom chambers of the heart, the ventricles, quit pumping blood and flutter some three times a minute. Several hundred thousand people in the United States suffer the same condition each year, and many of them could be saved if passersby knew CPR. Luckily I knew what to do. My sister-in-law Anne and I kept Gracie alive until the rescue squad got there and shocked her heart back into beating.

Within a few days, Gracie had an AICD implanted. This is an internal device slightly smaller than a Sony Walkman that is wired to her heart and monitors it. Whenever her heart loses its rhythm, a mild shock (she says it feels like she's been kicked by a horse) brings it back to normal. Gracie literally carries her own rescue team with her everywhere she goes. And that rescue squad, her AICD, is made by Medtronic of Minneapolis.

Founder Earl Bakken started Medtronic in his garage as a partnership in 1949 with the late Palmer J. Hermundslie and was chairman of the board until 1989. (They moved out of Hermundslie's garage in 1961.) With a background in electrical engineering, the two repaired electronic hospital equipment, but in the 1950s teamed up with a pioneer in open-heart surgery, Dr. C. Walton Lillehei, to develop a nine-volt battery-powered pacemaker for young heart patients. Shortly after that pacemakers were applied to some elderly patients with great success, and the company took off.

Over the past decade or so, Medtronic has expanded from pacemakers into one of the largest medical-device companies in the world. Across a dozen product categories, the company is a leader in more than half. Since 1986 sales increased more than 17 percent a year, with earnings growing at 25 percent. Doing business in seventeen countries, nonunionized Medtronic has no special parking places, company cars, country-club memberships, or other such frills.

The company insists that the subsequent generation of any of its medical devices, including my daughter's defibrillator, "produce better outcomes and lower the overall cost of treatment." The first internal defibrillator, the PCD, was implanted by Medtronic in May 1989. The design cycle to produce the successor, the Jewel, took thirty-one months, then fourteen months to produce the Jewel

Plus, twelve for the Micro Jewel, nine for the Micro Jewel II, and just four for the Jewel AF, which came on the market in January 1997.

Thanks to Earl Bakken and Medtronic, thousands of people across the globe live longer and fuller lives. I give special thanks for their allowing Gracie to live a normal life.

Having studied and analyzed hundreds of the enterprises in America's Finest Companies, I learned they share the following traits:

1. The finest companies serve customers and employees with a passion.
2. Their managements are strong and decisive.
3. Each company knows where it wants to go.
4. They carve out their own paths for growth.
5. The companies are creative and innovative.
6. They carefully control expenses.
7. They respond to problems rather than react to them.

If you invest exclusively in the companies in America's Finest Companies, you'll be putting these traits to work for you in your portfolio. If the historic performance of their stocks continues, you'll do far better than most professional money managers.

CHAPTER FIVE

Where Are the Customers' Yachts?

William R. Travers was a well-known nineteenth-century lawyer who regularly used to visit swank Newport, Rhode Island. J. P. Morgan, John D. Rockefeller, and other notable Wall Street financiers and millionaire industrialists built "cottages" (we call them mansions today) there for weekend and summer retreats. Yacht racing was the sport of that day, and Travers was present at all the best events. One Sunday he was in a small group at the finish line watching yacht after yacht glide across. As names of the owners were announced, Travers noticed each one was a wealthy stockbroker. While staring at the fancy flotilla, Travers, a stutterer, shouted out, "And w-w-where are the c-c-customers' yachts?"

Fred Schwed, Jr., wrote best-selling *Wacky, the Small Boy* in 1939. In the About the Author section, Schwed was said to have "attended Lawrenceville and Princeton and has spent the last ten years in Wall Street. As a result he knows everything there is to know about children." That doesn't say much about Schwed's forte in the financial arena, but it does give you a good idea of the terrific sense of humor he had. Schwed was an early skeptic of Wall Street and decided to write *Where Are the Customers' Yachts?* (or *A Good Hard Look at Wall Street*) to share his witty wisdom. He got Simon & Schuster to publish it in 1940. The book has been successful enough to have been reprinted several times since.

Schwed's opening reminds the reader that Wall Street has a river at one end and a graveyard at the other. Schwed said he viewed Wall Street's daily activities from a trading table with every conceivable form of communication except the heliograph. In such an enviable position, he was "constantly exchanging . . . quotations, orders, bluffs, fibs, lies and nonsense." Having observed all this for at least a decade, Schwed decided to dedicate his book to examining the nonsense, "a commodity which keeps sluicing in through the weeks and years with the irresistible constancy of the waters of the rolling Mississippi."

I particularly liked his discussion of investment trusts, which were the forerunners of modern-day mutual funds. They were formed under the assumption that

> the average individual is incapable of handling his own financial destiny. What is worse, he cannot, unless he is very

rich, purchase the best financial advice. (We are assuming for the moment that there is such a thing as the best financial advice.)

So a lot of us who clearly are not magicians pool our money and hire a set of professional experts to do the guessing. They may not be quite magicians but they have everything that should be necessary—experience, reputation, trained staffs, inside information, and unlimited resources for research. Since the amount we pool together is often in the neighborhood of a hundred million dollars, we can afford to pay them fortunes for their ability. Paying them fortunes will be a great bargain for us, provided only that they come across with the ability.

One would think they could do this, or at least do it better than we could. If investment trusts would only function in actuality anything like as well as they do in theory, they would be a tremendous asset to the general welfare.

Schwed believed most investment professionals aren't dishonest. They're simply inept. He wrote, "This book has chiefly tried to paint a picture of thousands of erring humans, of varying degrees of good will, solemnly engaged in the business of predicting the unpredictable. To this effort most of them bring a certain cockeyed sincerity." I agree with Schwed.

Since I started my newsletter, *The Staton Institute*ˢᴹ *Advisory,* twelve years ago, I've amassed a thick file of evidence that proves that the large majority of professional money managers, the experts millions of people rely upon to help their money grow, consistently underperform the stock market. The file is more than two inches thick and growing. It's jam-packed with articles from all sorts of places, but for the most part they're straight from everyday business and financial journals, including *The Wall Street*

Journal, Forbes, Fortune, Business Week, and *Financial World.* I haven't gone out of my way to obtain the evidence. It comes regularly and frequently in my mail.

Before I explain why most professionals cannot beat the market on a regular basis, I want to show you some recent evidence of the poor job they're doing:

1. One might expect that our investment judgments, given our training and experience, would prove sound and profitable for our clients. But this is, strikingly, not true.

    —ARNOLD S. WOOD, PRESIDENT
    MARTINGALE ASSET MANAGEMENT
    FINANCIAL ANALYSTS JOURNAL, MAY–JUNE 1989

2. In the 10-year period ending December 1988, SEI, a pension fund consulting firm, found only 40 percent of all pension funds were able to beat the S & P 500 at least half the time. Only one manager in 100 beat the market in each of 10 years, and only one manager in 50 beat the market in each of five years.

    —*THE FINANCIAL WEEKLY,* JANUARY 29, 1990

3. Seventy-five percent of all professional money managers fail to beat the market in any given period, according to studies done by Ibbotson Associates of Chicago, an investment research firm.

    —*FINANCIAL WORLD,* MAY 1, 1990

4. Since 1969, the unmanaged S & P 500-stock index has handily outgained the average stock fund, ris-

ing 680% vs. 550%. Ten thousand dollars invested on Jan. 1, 1969, in a portfolio that matched the S & P would have grown to $78,600 last Jan. 1. The same amount in the average stock fund: $65,800.

—*MONEY*, MAY 1991

5. Of the more than 1,000 equity mutual funds in existence, only a handful have beaten the market over the past 10 years.

    —*THE MUTUAL FUND LETTER*, JULY 1991

6. Of the 41 domestic equity funds managed by Merrill Lynch, Shearson, Paine Webber, Dean Witter and Prudential Securities, only 2 have beaten the market since 1988. Over the period, not one of these five brokerage firm families outperformed the S & P 500.

    —*FORBES*, SEPTEMBER 2, 1991

7. Many of the 400 or so investor newsletters aren't worth the price of a subscription, which can run $500 or more a year.

    —*FORTUNE*, SEPTEMBER 23, 1991

8. Only four services [investment letters] outperformed the Wilshire 5000 over the 11½-year period [6/30/80–12/31/91], which shows you how tough it is to beat the market.

    —*THE CHARTIST*, FEBRUARY 6, 1992

9. "About one fifth of the investment letter universe appears to beat the market over the long term," says Hulbert, pointing out that less then 20% of all mutual funds outperform the market.

    —INTERVIEW WITH MARK HULBERT, PUBLISHER OF *HULBERT'S FINANCIAL DIGEST* IN *FORBES*, SEPTEMBER 14, 1992

10. The average stock mutual fund climbed just 7.89% in the year [1992] through Dec. 23, slightly behind the Standard & Poor's 500-Stock Index.

    —*THE WALL STREET JOURNAL*, JANUARY 4, 1993

11. According to Lipper Analytical, stock funds returned 13.5% a year over the 10 years through December [1992], compared with 16.2% for the Standard & Poor's 500-Stock Index.

    —*THE WALL STREET JOURNAL*, MARCH 5, 1993

12. By and large, professional investors do a mediocre job of stock-picking. That, along with their expenses and fees, causes them to lag well behind the market.

    —*BUSINESS WEEK*, MAY 31, 1993

13. Overall, money managers have done a dismal job.

    —*FORTUNE*, OCTOBER 31, 1994

14. Over the last decade, according to Lipper Analytical Services, just 21% of mutual funds with a U.S. equity focus did better than an index fund.

    —*FORBES*, SEPTEMBER 25, 1995

15. There is not a single academic study . . . that suggests that active manager performance is anything more than the expected distribution around the mean. And, since fund managers charge for their services, the mean will always be below the indexes. The great majority of active funds fail to outperform the indexes.

—*FEE ADVISOR,* NOVEMBER/DECEMBER 1995

16. Of the nearly 500 portfolios among 152 letters tracked by *Hulbert Financial Digest,* only 45 matched the 37.5% total return of Standard & Poor's 500-stock index in 1995.

—*KIPLINGER'S PERSONAL FINANCE MAGAZINE,* APRIL 1996

Mutual funds have become the most popular way for individuals to invest. There are now in excess of 9,000 different mutual funds, with more than $7 trillion in assets at the end of 1996. About 3,500+ of them invest in stocks. With so much money on the line and pouring into the equity funds at a record clip, you'd think investors would be more careful about where they put their money. But they are often lured by the creative advertising of mutual funds, which seem to offer so much and in reality frequently produce so little. Thumb through any of dozens of investment publications, and you'll see ads for this fund or that. Note how they tout their "outstanding" records. One of my money-manager friends (who actually does beat the market) wryly noted, "Every money manager in the country says he's in the top 25 percent." But we know that's an impossibility.

Since so few professionals, whether they be investment counselors, pension-fund managers, or mutual-fund managers, beat the market, investors need to understand why so they don't make the same mistakes the pros make. Financial institutions control about 80 percent of all trading volume on the New York Stock Exchange. On an average day some 200 to 300 million shares are bought and sold. Individuals account for 20 percent of that.

Vilfredo Pareto was an Italian sociologist and economist for whom the famous Pareto Principle is named. After observing thousands of workers in hundreds of businesses from the late nineteenth through the early twentieth century, he concluded that 80 percent of results comes from 20 percent of effort. To say it another way, 20 percent of an advertising budget results in 80 percent of the incremental revenue. Twenty percent of a day's work produces 80 percent of the benefits of that work. The top 20 percent of workers in any organization typically produce about 80 percent of sales and earnings. Although no results will divide exactly into 20/80, it's an excellent rule of thumb. And it's interesting to me that NYSE volume is now almost exactly 20 percent by individuals and 80 percent by financial institutions. As you've already seen, the 80 percent produces subpar results, which implies the 20 percent— individual investors—produces superior results.

I profiled Benjamin Graham, the father of modern-day securities analysis, in chapter 3 and provided excerpts from the final interview he gave shortly before his death. In just ten sentences, Graham ripped apart the fantasy that the financial community can accurately predict short-term changes in the economy and stock prices. He also reasoned that the stock-market experts can't continuously beat the market because they are the market. You can't beat the average when you are the average.

On the other hand, "The typical individual investor," he said later in the interview, "has a great advantage over the large institutions." As I'll demonstrate, that advantage can lead you to above-average profits if you create and manage your own portfolio made up of America's Finest Companies.

I don't want you to think I'm bashing all professional money managers and advisors. For the record, I am not against professional advice or money management. I *am* against paying a so-called expert for subpar performance, something far too many individuals are doing. In fairness to the pros, though, their customers help create these inferior results. Here's how.

For whatever reasons—lack of time, no investment background, personal finance seeming too complicated—many people believe they can't manage their own money well. Since they have no confidence in their own ability, they turn to experts to take care of their money for them. An expert is defined as one "displaying special skill or knowledge derived from training and experience." Millions of people believe there are a large number of stock-market experts who earn superior investment returns, primarily through accurate forecasting and making savvy moves into and out of stocks. Even though this is a widely held belief, as you've already seen, it's false.

Investors must pay annual fees for services from trust departments, investment counselors, and mutual funds. If they use brokers, the brokers will charge a commission for each transaction. If they use financial planners, they'll pay fees and/or sales loads on the various financial products offered by the planners. Anywhere investors turn there's a charge for advice and management unless they choose to do it themselves. What pro in his right mind would manage money for free?

When investors pay to have their money managed, they expect the professionals they're paying to earn their keep by studying the economy and stock market, by buying and selling when the time is ripe, and by going into cash in case the market should go down. Isn't that right? Would you pay an expert to spend little of his time taking care of your money? Of course not. You want that expert to be working—and working hard—on your behalf. You want that expert to spend as much time with your money as he can, and because you want that, he does what you expect.

Professionals rely heavily on forecasts of expected performance of the economy, the stock market, and individual companies. That's not too surprising because forecasting, especially of the economy, has been in existence for centuries. People from all walks of life are attracted to it. Everyone wants that special peek ahead. When Marco Polo returned to his homeland from the Orient, he told of kites used as economic-forecasting devices. Before a merchant ship embarked on a trading voyage, a drunkard (you had to be drunk to do this) was tied to a kite and launched from the ship's deck. If, and it was a big if, the drunkard actually made it into the air, the voyage was expected to be successful. But if he crashed, the trip was postponed if not canceled.

Despite the awesome academic evidence that forecasts are usually wrong (because no one can see into the future), many money managers continue to defy logic and rationality. It's not really mysterious, though, when you consider that millions of people still smoke and chew tobacco, although they know that tobacco is harmful; or continue to gamble at the racetrack, in lotteries, or Las Vegas, although the house wins 99 percent of the time; or abuse drugs; or drive without seat belts fastened. Each money manager believes he has found the forecast (or forecasts) that will allow him to gaze profitably into the future, even though his counterparts won't be successful.

Let me take you on a brief journey through history to show you some of the most widely heralded predictions about the economy and stock market made by acclaimed experts:

1. Stocks have reached what looks like a permanently high plateau.

   —IRVING FISHER, PROFESSOR OF ECONOMICS AT YALE, OCTOBER 17, 1929

   Seven days later, on October 24, panic struck Wall Street and stock values plummeted.

2. The end of the decline of the Stock Market . . . will probably not be long, only a few more days at most.

   —IRVING FISHER TRYING TO REGAIN SOME OF HIS LOST LUSTER, NOVEMBER 14, 1929

   Nice try, Irving.

3. Financial storm definitely passed.

   —CABLEGRAM TO WINSTON CHURCHILL FROM BERNARD BARUCH, NOVEMBER 15, 1929

   Security prices had just begun their freefall into 1932.

4. Gentlemen, you have come sixty days too late. The Depression is over.

> —HERBERT HOOVER RESPONDING TO A
> DELEGATION REQUESTING A PUBLIC-WORKS
> PROGRAM TO HELP SPEED THE RECOVERY, JUNE
> 1930

What recovery? The economy hadn't come close to bottoming.

5. During the next four years . . . unless drastic steps are taken by Congress, the U.S. will have nearly 8,000,000 unemployed and will stand on the brink of a deep depression.

> —HENRY C. WALLACE, U.S. SECRETARY OF
> COMMERCE, NOVEMBER 1945

Between 1945 and 1950, U.S. GNP rose nearly 50 percent.

6. Nineteen sixty promises to be the most prosperous [year] in our history.

> —ROBERT A. ANDERSON, U.S. SECRETARY OF THE
> TREASURY, APRIL 14, 1960

Business conditions will stay good for some time to come. We are not about to enter any sharp recession.

> —HENRY C. ALEXANDER, CHAIRMAN OF THE
> MORGAN GUARANTY TRUST COMPANY, APRIL 22,
> 1960

The recession of 1960 began that same month.

7. There ain't going to be no recession. I guarantee it.

—PIERRE RINFRET, POPULAR ECONOMIST AND
INVESTMENT COUNSELOR, APRIL 1969

The 1969–71 recession started the following summer.

8. There will be no recession in the United States of America.

—RICHARD NIXON, PRESIDENT, STATE OF THE
UNION ADDRESS, 1974

The GNP dropped 5.8 percent the first quarter of 1974, and by July the economy was (you guessed it) in the deepest recession since the 1930s.

9. A drastic reduction in the deficit . . . will take place in the fiscal year '82.

—RONALD REAGAN, PRESIDENT, MARCH 1981

In fiscal 1982, the government had a record deficit up to that time—$110.7 billion.

10. A grim first quarter is projected for stocks.

—*WALL STREET JOURNAL* HEADLINE, JANUARY 3,
1995

Not only was the first quarter one of the strongest for stocks in history, so was the entire year 1995.

Will Rogers once said, "An economist's guess is liable to be as good as anyone else's." In spring 1990, the National

Association of Business Economists (whose main function seems to be polling itself) "guessed" that the remainder of the year and the several beyond it would be good. Specifically, 80 percent of the members predicted no recession for 1990, while 67 percent said there wouldn't be one of these nasty little events for at least three more years. In response to their pool, supercolumnist Alan Abelson of *Barron's* wrote, "Near-unanimity in this case breeds contempt. Anyone with even a taint of contrarian blood can only pray that, please, Lord, just this once, let 68 economists be right." Despite Abelson's plea, the economists were dead wrong. The deep recession of 1990–91 began shortly after the NABE pool was released.

For the twelve years from the end of 1982 through 1994, the consensus prediction of economists polled by *The Wall Street Journal* missed the change of direction in interest rates 18 of 25 times, an error ratio of 72 percent. So-called "professional" stock analysts fared even worse. According to *Worth* magazine's "1996 Investing Guide," analysts failed to see the earnings downturns heading into the 1981 recession, the slowdown of 1984–86, and the subsequent recession of 1990 too.

These are only a few examples of predictions that were way wide of the mark. I could provide hundreds of others, many of which in retrospect are quite humorous, but I think I've proved a point. David Dreman, author of *The New Contrarian Investment Strategy*, said, "Expert opinion—which investors naturally rely on—is very often wrong and not infrequently dramatically so." He devotes page after page to detailing the poor performance of the experts who try in vain to predict accurately.

If the evidence is so overwhelming that economic and

stock-market forecasting is a fool's game, why do people rely on it so heavily? Eric Hoffer believed society is addicted to pollsters and forecasters. "Even when the forecasts prove wrong, we still go on asking for them. We watch our experts read the entrails of statistical tables and graphs the way the ancients watched the soothsayers read the entrails of a chicken."

The final word on why forecasting is so often awry comes from *The Futurist* magazine (January–February 1990):

> Forecasts that a current trend will continue indefinitely are generally wrong, since most trends eventually reach a constraint.
>
> Forecasts that describe ominous doom are frequently wrong, since society usually addresses a problem once it has been identified as being critical.
>
> Forecasts that describe a traditional solution to a critical problem are usually wrong. Society seems to find creative and innovative solutions.

The Futurist wasn't completely negative on forecasting. They believe forecasting can be much improved if it's based on analogy. The forecaster looks at past developments and sees how a similar sequence of events might happen in the future. That's the technique I've successfully used for years as an economic historian and superior stock picker.

Professional money managers try to make a perfect science of forecasting and investing. If they put A into a computer, they expect B to come out. Although B always follows A in the alphabet, it doesn't always follow A out of a computer. Thinking and acting this way creates frequent mistakes. No one knows where the Dow or the S & P 500 will be a year from now. No one knows how much money any company will earn in 1995. No one knows how strong the economy will be. Yet much of the typical professional's time is involved in trying to find the answers, all for nought.

Bennett W. Goodspeed, who in his own words "overcame the handicaps of having an MBA and working for several prominent Wall Street firms," wrote *The Tao Jones Averages: A Guide to Whole-Brained Investing* in 1983. It's a fascinating little book (154 pages). Goodspeed said analysts and portfolio managers "create an overload of information in their frenzied activity." I call it Paralysis of Overanalysis. Overload is harmful. In the words of the Chinese philosopher Lao-tzu, "The more stuffed the mind is with knowledge, the less able one can see what's in front of him."

Even if their forecasts for the economy and direction of the stock market were always on the money, most professional money managers would still rarely beat the market. The reason is the market has no operating expenses, but the professional does. Expenses eat sharply into returns.

Even to duplicate the market (not try to outperform it), the money manager has to trade frequently. Because stocks change multiple times in value every day, at any given time each stock in the Dow, the S & P 500, the Wilshire 5000, or any other market index he's trying to copy changes in its proportional weighting to all the others in the index. The cost of buying and selling to keep stocks in correct proportion (although that's not the only reason) almost singly guarantees that attempts to mimic the market will fail.

There are other excellent reasons why most professionals can't match the market. One is cash. Mutual funds have to keep cash available for customers who wish to redeem shares. That amount usually ranges between 5 percent when they're optimistic on stock prices and 10 to 15 percent when they're negative. On any given day they must have reserve in case more of their customers want to redeem shares than buy them. The fund manager doesn't want to be forced to sell part of his portfolio to pay for these redeemed shares. He always opts to dip into the cash reserve. For the long term, stocks earn three to four times as much as cash. The higher the fund's cash reserve, the more its return is penalized. Every fund has such a reserve, and every fund is damaged by it. The individual doesn't need a cash kitty, so his results aren't impacted.

Still another problem for money managers, including mutual funds, is forced panic selling. During the Great Crash of 1987, mutual funds were bombarded with so many redemptions they had to sell even though they may not have wanted to. Fortunately their phone lines were jammed with panicked callers. Otherwise they would have had to sell even more of their portfolios. This unplanned selling occurred, you guessed it, at or near the bottom. Once the chaos subsided, they had to reinvest at higher prices.

On Black Monday, October 19, I mailed a one-page memo to all my clients urging them to stand pat because there was blood in the streets, and you never sell when the blood is running. This is one Wall Street maxim that's true. I also told them to wait a few days for orderly trading to resume and then add to their portfolios. Those who heeded my advice not only recovered all their paper losses but also added greatly to their coffers. Mutual funds were forced to react. Savvy individuals responded and took advantage of what looked like a horrible situation but was in reality one of the premier buying opportunities in history.

When a financial institution (I include mutual funds) buys or sells shares of a company, it normally does so at various prices. Their buying and selling power is so enormous it affects their own transactions. Let's say you and a money manager hear on *Wall Street Week* a great idea that sparks new interest in an underfollowed New York Stock Exchange (NYSE) company that doesn't trade in big volume. The following Monday you call your broker to buy 100 shares, and the price is 28 (remember: stock prices don't need the dollar sign). For $2,800 plus commission you own the stock. At the same time, the money manager calls his broker and wants to buy 10,000 shares. He gets the first 2,000 at 28, the next 3,000 at 29, 3,000 more at 29½, and the final 2,000 at 30.

Three years later the same analyst who recommended that stock is on *Wall Street Week* saying sell it. Coincidentally, you and the money manager are watching the show and both decide to sell on money. You call your broker and get out of your 100 shares at 42 less commission. The manager calls his broker and sells 3,000 at 42. Stock prices happen to be very weak that day, so the specialist handling the order on the NYSE takes the stock down a point on the next 3,000. Then he knocks it another 1½ points and clears the remaining 4,000 shares.

In both of these situations, which aren't unusual, the fund's average cost to buy is higher than the individual's. The fund's proceeds from selling are lower. Financial institutions deal in thousands and tens of thousands of shares. Their buying and selling can drive stocks up or down before they complete their orders. It can take days if not weeks to accumulate or unload a position, whereas the individual can get in or out with one phone call with the price sometimes confirmed before he hangs up. This is another reason professionals have a tough time equaling or beating the market.

The Wall Street Journal asks, "How much does it really cost to have someone manage your money?

> Money managers and investment advisers all quote rates that seem straightforward enough. But the price that they give for their hand-holding usually doesn't include a variety of other charges investors typically end up paying. These include brokerage-firm trading costs to buy and sell stocks during the year and management and administration fees levied by mutual fund companies. There is also the cost of setting up a new portfolio in the first place.
>
> The differences in total costs can be huge. Depending on the adviser's investment style, total annual costs can range from a low of about 1% of assets under management to 4%, or more. Initial costs of setting up a portfolio can run from less than 1% of the portfolio to 10% or more.

For the rest of this chapter, I'll stick solely to the costs involved with mutual funds, since this book is about creating your own mini-mutual fund and outpacing most existing funds. The first cost I'll discuss is the load. That's the charge you may incur to buy or redeem a fund's shares. No-load mutual funds don't charge anything, and they make up about half the equity funds.

The other half is load funds. Their load go up to 8.5 percent, although that's extreme. The industry average is 3–4 percent. Most loads are front-end. They're deducted before you invest in the fund. A few funds have back-end loads that are taken out only when you redeem your shares. The top twenty-five general equity funds, led by Fidelity Magellan, have more than $700 billion under management. Fifteen have loads.

The services rating mutual-fund total returns—capital appreciation with dividends reinvested—don't take loads into account. That makes comparing load funds to no-loads a more difficult chore, but there's one thing for certain. If a load fund and a no-load fund have exactly the same rates of return, the no-load will put more money into your pocket.

Taxes are another bugaboo. The performance-rating services usually don't consider them either. If your mutual funds are in a retirement account, taxes aren't a problem. But since the bulk of mutual funds is in taxable accounts, taxes are a sad reality. They can cripple returns, particularly if you're in a high tax bracket.

The Wall Street Journal wrote, "Beware Tax Consequences of Mutual Funds" in the February 22, 1992, edition. "Would you like to pay taxes on somebody else's gains? How about paying your taxes years earlier than you have to? Most people would answer both questions with a resounding 'No.' But mutual fund investors frequently subject themselves to such taxing situations, often without being aware of it." The *Journal* calculated how negatively taxes affected returns of the top ten mutual funds for the decade ending December 31, 1991.

Taxes took away one-quarter of the average total return during the ten years. That's a huge bite, a bite that could be completely eliminated if you assemble your own mini-mutual fund. As your own money manager, you control when to realize a capital gain; therefore, you control when to pay taxes on a gain. If you're in a mutual fund, that's a choice you don't have.

The National Bureau of Economic Research released its study "Ranking Mutual Funds on an After-Tax Basis" by economics professors Joel M. Dickson and John B. Shoven of Stanford University. Their study covered sixty-two growth and growth-and-income mutual funds with thirty-year records from 1963 to 1992 on a pretax and aftertax basis. One dollar invested in the Standard & Poor's 500 index in 1963 grew to $22.13 by the end of 1992. The median result for the sixty-two funds was that one dollar grew to $21.89 over the same period. Thus, the typical fund underperformed the stock market over the three decades, and that was before taxes. After taxes, the results were much worse.

For the thirty years, one dollar invested by an individual in a low-tax bracket grew to $16.45. The same dollar invested by someone in a medium-tax bracket grew to $12.82, while someone in the highest-tax bracket saw his dollar grow to just $9.87. Taxes took away 24.9 percent of the low-tax investor's return; 41.4 percent of the medium-tax investor's return; and a whopping 55 percent of the high-tax investor's return.

If taxes and loads aren't enough heavy yokes on the investor's shoulders, there are also annual administrative expenses and the management fee to consider. Mutual-fund administrative expenses range from ½ percent to 1½ percent of assets. Yearly management fees are in the same range. Together they cost the investor between 1 and 3 percent of total assets under management.

And finally there are trading costs. According to *Forbes* (November 23, 1992), "Turnover is, like the annual expense ratio, one of those numbers that fund vendors are compelled to disclose [in prospectuses] but that buyers all too often ignore. Just how great are transaction costs? Higher than you might think. A round-trip trade (a sell and a buy) executed on one of the stock exchanges probably costs a fund at least 0.35 percent of the transaction amount; for small, illiquid Nasdaq stocks the cost is closer to 1 percent. That's an annual cost of 1 percent to 3 percent for a fund reporting a 300 percent turnover." Even the best of funds have high turnover rates. That is, they literally sell and rebuy the equivalent value of the entire portfolio one or more times every year. Each time they buy and sell, two commissions—no matter how small—are paid. And those commissions eat into the investor's return.

The most recent evidence is just as damaging if not more so. According to the April 1996 edition of *Smart Money*, two-thirds of all funds charge the notorious 12b-1 fee ("whose existence is buried somewhere in the prospectus"), which can range up to 1 percent of assets each year even in so-called "no-load" mutual funds. Frequently part of this fee is directed to stockbrokers and money managers as incentive to sell a particular fund. The downside is that the portion paid to a broker may incite him to keep you in a fund even if it's doing poorly. Another portion of the fee can pay for advertising and marketing a fund.

A recent study by Morningstar concludes that the average fund loses 0.3 percent of its annual value to commissions but, depending on the activity in the fund, might surrender up to 1 percent of asset value every year. This "loss" comes out of the investor's pocket, not the fund's.

Despite a plethora of mutual funds of every kind, hence more intense competition, *Kiplinger's Personal Finance* magazine (April 1996) notes that the total expense ratio of the average diversified U.S. stock fund "has risen a dramatic 44 percent since 1980." Sadly *The Wall Street Journal* (December 1, 1995) says that "figuring out how much you really pay for your funds is more difficult. Many investors are getting soaked."

The Journal (July 22, 1997) also notes that the majority of taxable stock funds are run with "scant regard" for their shareholders. They figure that to overcome taxes and other investment costs, the typical stock fund would have to beat a tax-managed fund (run to minimize taxes) by 2.63 percentage points per year. What are the odds of that? Very slim.

· The July 14, 1997, issue of *Barron's* observed that for the year to date (through July 3, 1997), twelve months, and thirty-six months, the percentage of stock funds beating the S&P 500 was 3.9, 5.6, and 5 respectively.

With so many different costs associated with mutual funds, it gets confusing trying to see how they impact on returns. So I've put together a simple example that shows the hypothetical returns from Jazzy Fund versus Standard & Poor's 500 index for the next five years in a taxable account. You've already seen that most equity mutual funds can't equal the market (and that's before loads and taxes are considered), but to make this really interesting I've given the fund the return advantage. I assume Jazzy Fund will grow at 14 percent annually with the S & P 500 growing at 11 percent, one percentage point under its historic average.

Jazzy is a low-yield fund, so its return will be 2 percent from dividends and 12 percent from appreciation. S & P's total annual return will be 4 percent from dividends and 7 percent from appreciation, which is roughly the historic norm. One thousand dollars will be invested in the fund and the S & P index at the beginning of each of the five years. For ease of comparison, I assume no sales load to buy the fund nor any commission to buy the S & P, and the investor in either is in the combined 35 percent tax bracket—28 percent federal and 7 percent state.

According to *Business Week* and a number of other reputable financial publications, mutual-fund returns in taxable accounts are 30–40 percent lower when both federal and state taxes are taken into account. Economists Shoven and Dickson said the take could be a lot more, so I'm being perhaps a little too biased in favor of mutual funds with this example.

At the beginning of year one, $1,000 goes into Jazzy. During the year, $20 (2 percent) is paid out in dividends. After taxes at 35 percent, $13 is left. The fund rises 12 percent in value to $1,120 and like so many funds turns the portfolio exactly one time. This means the $120 gain is taxed at 35 percent, leaving a net gain of $78 for a total of $1,078. The fund charges a 1 percent management fee and another 1 percent for expenses. Those come out of the $1,078 leaving $1,056 after all expenses and taxes. Adding back in the $13 in dividends, $1,069 is left. That's a 6.9 percent net return.

One thousand dollars also goes into the S & P 500 at the beginning of the year. During the year the S & P pays $40 (4 percent) in dividends. After taxes $26 is left. The fund rises 7 percent in value to $1,070. There is no turnover, hence no capital gain, so the entire $1,070 is left. Add back in the $26 in dividends and the amount is $1,096, a 9.6 percent net return.

At the beginning of each of the next four years, $1,000 is added to both accounts. And the scenario above repeats each time. Please see the table below.

Even though Jazzy Fund earns three percentage points more than the S & P every year, the S & P does better because there is no selling, hence no capital-gains taxes. If we continue the exercise, at the end of year ten the difference will be even more startling. Jazzy Fund will have grown to $14,701. The S & P will have swelled to $17,134.

Of course, you can argue this is an unfair comparison because the Jazzy Fund investor has already paid his taxes, and taxes are still owed by the investor who owns the "market." That's true to a degree but not as much as you may think. I have compared the S & P 500 index to a fund that outperforms it, a circumstance that doesn't happen too often.

You're going to learn how to build your own mini-mutual fund that will consistently outdistance the market indexes. That's one reason capital-gains taxes won't be a hindrance. The other is almost all the mutual funds you'll compare your results to won't beat the indexes as in the example above. They'll be behind.

Benjamin Graham was right when he said the individual

	VALUE OF JAZZY FUND	VALUE OF S & P 500
End of Year 1	$1,069	$1,096
End of Year 2	2,212	2,297
End of Year 3	3,434	3,614
End of Year 4	4,740	5,056
End of Year 5	6,136	6,637

has many advantages over the financial institutions. One major advantage is that you, the individual, can control your own financial destiny rather than be at the mercy of someone else. The other major advantage is that you can assemble your own equity mini-mutual fund, equal or beat the market year in and year out, and outperform 75 percent of the investment professionals. Then, it won't be just the stockbrokers and other investment pros who can afford to buy yachts. You'll be able to afford one, too.

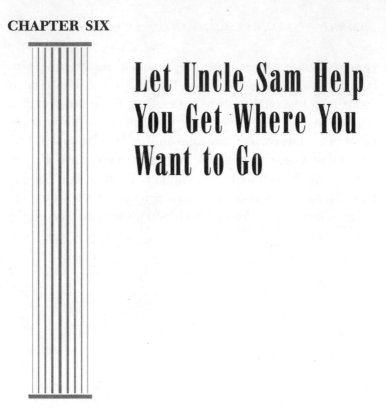

CHAPTER SIX

Let Uncle Sam Help You Get Where You Want to Go

The reward of energy, enterprise and thrift—is taxes.

—WILLIAM FEATHER

For most families, the two most important financial goals are educating children and having enough money to live comfortably in retirement. I prefer to call if life after work because retiring has connotations of being old and inactive, when the opposite is usually true. If a man or woman reaches age sixty to sixty-five in good health, odds are very high he or she will live at least another twenty years. One of the biggest problems older people in this country face is living a long, healthy life but not having enough money to travel and do whatever else they wish in their later years.

The typical married couple reaching age sixty-five has about $7,000 in liquid assets in addition to Social Security benefits and possible home ownership. At the rate you're spending money today, how long would $7,000 last? Two months? Three months? Four months? I doubt it would be beyond four months if that long.

Having enough money for life after work is easily achievable when you start early enough and invest your money on a regular basis. If you've already started, that's great. If not, it's still not too late, and you have lots of company. *Money* magazine conducted a survey a few years ago and discovered one of four people between ages forty-five and sixty-five has set aside nothing for life after work. Three out of four said they hadn't saved enough to live in the style they desired, and nearly one of two said their biggest fear was not having enough money to carry them through life after work. Those that were preparing for life after work said their preferred investment was a savings account, which historically has not kept up with inflation and taxes. Just 25 percent bought shares of stock, the best inflation hedge of all.

It's easy to see why so many people aren't prepared for life after work. If you're in your twenties or thirties, you're still some thirty to forty years away. Even if you're fifty, as I am, it will still be a decade and a half before you reach sixty-five. Somehow twenty, thirty, or forty years seems so far away we imagine there's still plenty of time to get ready for life after work, so why worry about it now? That's the way all those who haven't begun planning think. If they don't think that way, then why haven't they started?

Another reason people don't get ready for life after work is they don't save any money. All their income is spent to pay the grocer, the mortgage company, the auto dealer, the department store, the phone company, the local utility, the doctor, the TV repairman, the movie theater, the video-rental store. The list goes on and on. These people spend every dollar they make. Sometimes they spend more than they make and borrow to make up the difference. They reason that one day they'll start to save some money as soon as they quit spending so much. But few really ever do it. It's a fantasy.

To be able to invest, you've got to be able to save. The first place you ought to invest your savings is in a retirement plan. The only way you'll be able to invest in a retirement plan is to budget for it using my formula.

As a teenager I read the wonderful story in Norman Vincent Peale's *Guideposts* magazine about Joseph Colgate, founder of the forerunner of Colgate-Palmolive and Colgate University. Mr. Colgate's business was so successful he quickly turned into a multimillionaire and decided he had far more money than he needed. So he started giving it away.

He first gave away 10 percent of each year's income, but after he started giving his income multiplied. He then upped the percentage to 15, and the same thing happened again. Next he gave away 20 percent of his income, but money poured into his coffers like water through a broken dam. After studying his "problem," Mr. Colgate finally turned his money over to a foundation and let others figure out what to do with it. Giving away his money created a giant hole which was then refilled with even more money than before.

In my business and personal lives, I operate under an amazingly simple formula:

100% of my income
less: some income for me
less: some income for others
spend: everything else

Americans who don't do well with their money use a different formula. When money comes in they spend it on everybody they can think of—the grocer, the utility company, the mortgage company, the car company, the clothier, the department store, the hardware, the water company—and if, and this is a big if, there's any money left they'll use it for their financial future. The dilemma is that there's never anything left because they don't plan for any to be.

If somebody says, "I'll try to do it," what are the odds he'll do it as compared with if he says, "I will do it." You can't try to do anything. Either you do it or you don't. You can't try to save money for your future. Either you do it or you don't. There is no in between about saving money and because there isn't, people get trapped. Without actually paying themselves first, people rarely have any money left over to save and invest.

Any couple can easily save $600 a year by putting pocket change into a jar at the end of a day and taking it to the bank at the end of each month. Six hundred dollars a year put into a handful of companies, in America's Finest Companies (and reinvesting all dividends), can be as much as $1.5 million at the end of forty years even though the total invested was just $24,000 scattered evenly over four decades.

Not only do I believe in paying myself first, I also believe in paying others first who need it. When I set aside pretax income for myself, I also set aside the same percentage for the charities, church, organizations, and causes I believe in. Joseph Colgate proved this works. Many others have proved it too.

I'm reminded of the story about a deep well with the purest, best-tasting water anyone for miles around had ever tasted. For generations the old well served all the descendants of a farming family and anyone else who wanted to partake of its goodness. Through drought after drought, the well always provided all the water the farmer, his family, and their animals ever needed. Not once did it ever run low.

During the Great Depression hard times hit, and the farmer had to sell his farm and move. The property stayed empty and the well unused for many years until finally a new family bought it. Even though they came from another county, they knew the reputation of the old well and its water.

When the family moved in and rushed to the well to sample its contents, they were shocked to find it completely dry. In great disbelief, they stared at each other and realized the terrible investment they'd made buying a farm with a dry well. What they hadn't realized was that a well needs to be used to keep the water flowing. The thousands of tiny rivulets that flow into the well's cavern will stop up just as blood will not circulate if veins and arteries become clogged.

And so it is with money. To do the most good, to help the most people, money must flow and must not be hoarded as Hetty Green hoarded it.

She could read the financial pages at age six. At age thirty she inherited her father's fortune and began trading on Wall Street with "bold audacity." It wasn't her looks but her fierce style that earned her the name, the Witch of Wall Street.

The Witch was so tightfisted she wore only a black dress (maybe because she had just one). To save soap, she seldom washed it. Working alone on the first floor of a bank from which she coerced free space (probably because she owned it), Green lived the life of a pauper. She bought *The Wall Street Journal*, read it, and then resold it each day.

Despite her brutal nature, she managed to marry and bear two children. Her son, Ned, hurt himself sledding, and Hetty took him to a charity ward where she was recognized as a multimillionaire who could easily afford a hospital. But she refused to pay, the wound became infected, and Ned's leg was amputated. She left her children $50 million each when she died of a stroke in 1916 after arguing over the price of milk.

Clint Murchison, Jr., the famous Texas wildcatter, had the right attitude about money. "Money is like manure. If you spread it around, it does a lot of good. But if you pile it up in one place, it stinks like hell."

James Redfield, author of *The Celestine Prophecy*, also has the right attitude. His book has sold more than three million copies despite the fact that the plot has been called "flaky" and all other sorts of unflattering names.

In a fall 1994 interview, Redfield said that when you view money as a scarce resource, you are locked into a scarcity mentality. "No matter how tight money is for you, if you don't open your hand and make it available, it'll be hard for you to get more. When you give, you create a void [like the old well] that is filled again. And [like Joseph Colgate] you always receive much more."

Redfield gave up his therapy practice, self-published 3,000 copies of his book, and traveled with his wife across the Southeast giving away copies. He sold 150,000 books that way before cutting a deal with Warner Books. Redfield has already made so much money he's set up a foundation to dispose of it.

I have a theory that good things—often unexpectedly great things—happen when people with a giving attitude "empty their glass." Only a completely empty glass can be totally replenished. One of Jesus' most famous parables is about the poor woman who gave her last two coins to help others. She trusted that even though she had no money, her needs would be met. And we must assume they were.

My mission is to reach everyone who will listen with the gospel (gospel means truth) of investing money to earn the highest return possible in the least time with least risk. I gladly give away my expertise to people who can't afford it without asking anything in return. The more I give the more I am rewarded, frequently in ways never anticipated. "What goes around comes around" is really true. We are all part of giant circle, 5.6 billion of us, and each one has a part to play. Every person has a way to serve. Serving is what being human is all about. To serve is to give. The more you give, the more you get. The hand that gives gathers.

Before spending all your income, first allocate a certain percentage for investment, for your financial future. The amount can be 1 percent of pretax income, 2 percent, 5 percent, 10 percent, or more. It's up to you. You need to start with some percentage, regardless of how small, and then gradually increase it as fast as you can. Once you decide on a percentage to invest, allocate that same percentage for giving to others. Logically, the larger your income, the larger percentage you'll set aside to invest and to give.

Andrew Carnegie, the steel magnate who was once the richest man in the world, said, "You want to know if you will be rich? The answer is 'Can you save money?' " I might add, "Rich in the broadest sense means having abundant supply. Money is only one part of that abundance, a tool to use and to use wisely. Giving, to me, is part of using money wisely by sharing our abundance with others."

Because I see so many adults failing to prepare for their financial futures, I have a strong sense of mission about teaching young people how to manage their money so they'll end up where they want to be financially. I know the earlier they start the easier it will be and the more likely they are to make it. Why? Because saving, investing, and giving are a habit, one of the best habits there is. Once a person adopts the saving-investing-giving habit, it's as hard to quit as smoking.

Each year I have the privilege of teaching Junior Achievement's superb applied economics course to juniors and seniors at my daughter's school. I always spend a lot of time on investing because that's the subject I know the most about. I've just completed my tenth year, and I think I learn more than the students do. These eager juniors and seniors tell me they "waste" between $10 and $15 per week. This is money that slips through their hands. They don't know where it goes. They just know it disappears.

The lesson I try to get across is that if they invest that "wasted" money in a retirement plan at 12 percent per year, the rate of return from stocks since World War II, they'll end up with $1 million or more. Even minors can have retirement plans, as I'll show later. And yes, it is possible to invest in a well-diversified portfolio of stocks with that small amount of money. I'll demonstrate how easy it is. You don't have to go the customary mutual-fund route and end up with inferior results.

By simply beginning to invest $50 per month at 12 percent in an individual retirement account (IRA)—and never increasing the amount—a 16-year-old will have $1,749,977 by the age of 65. If he waits until 18, the amount will be $1,377,071. By waiting two more years until age 20, he will have only $1,083,462. That's still more than a million dollars, but it's $666,515 less than the one who started at 16. The 16-year-old, who makes 48 more payments of $50 per month (a total of $2,400 extra) than the 20-year-old, will wind up with 62 percent more money at age 65. Clearly, the earlier you start investing, the more money you'll have when you need it.

A few years ago Theodore Johnson died in Delray Beach, Florida, at age ninety. Mr. Johnson never made more than $14,000 a year, working for United Parcel Service, but he invested a dollar or two in UPS stock every change he got. When he retired in 1952 his stock was worth $700,000. When he died it had mushroomed to $70 million, and he left more than half of it to help disadvantaged young people get educations. If a man who never made more than $14,000 in a single year can become a multimillionaire, so can you.

Two young people aged nineteen graduate from high school. Both begin to work and have annual incomes. Investor Smart (a graduate of one of my Junior Achievement classes) opens an IRA through a stockbroker and begins to salt away the annual maximum of $2,000. He makes his contributions at the beginning of each year. Investor Not As Smart (who wasn't in my class) decides to wait a few years to open his IRA.

Investor Smart contributes $2,000 annually from age 19 through age 26 and quits. After contributing a total of $16,000, he decides (wrongly, in my opinion) to make no more contributions until he begins to withdraw funds from his IRA at age 65.

Investor Not As Smart, at age 27, wakes up to the realization he needs to begin preparing for retirement. He opens an IRA through his stockbroker and contributes $2,000 per year from age 27 through age 65, all the while earning 12 percent (the stock market's historic return) annually on his money as does Investor Smart.

For brevity, I've not shown every year, but Investor Not As Smart contributes $78,000 over the thirty-nine years he contributes to his plan. Thus, he puts nearly five times more into his IRA than Investor Smart. But when both are sixty-five, Investor Smart has $818,786 more than Investor Not As Smart. Even if Investor Not As Smart continues to invest $2,000 per year forever, he will never catch up with Investor Smart, who committed just $16,000. This is the best example I know to demonstrate the power of investing early for a new home, vacation, college education, life after work, or whatever.

Life after work will require a lot more money for some than for others. What will it take for you? When I launched my financial coaching career, the accepted rule of thumb was that if you were living comfortably on what you made when you were close to retiring, it would cost about 60 percent of that amount once you quit work. The theory sounded plausible. Your children were grown and gone. Since you were in your sixties, you weren't as active as when you worked. You didn't eat out as frequently, didn't travel as often, didn't buy as many "things" as before, etc. I guess the "experts" who came up with the 60 percent figure assumed everyone who retired sat around and played cards, or if they were really active played rousing games of shuffleboard in between naps.

Today we know the truth. More and more older people are very active and mentally alert. Milton Berle, Bob Hope, and my great aunts, Dot and Gladys, immediately come to mind.

I'm reminded of what Eubie Blake, the famous jazz pianist, said on his hundredth birthday: "If I'd known I was going to live this long, I'd have taken better care of myself." He died at 104. Dot and Gladys have taken excellent care of themselves. Gladys is the oldest of eleven children and is now 96. Baby sister Dot is only 94. They both spend much of their summers at Maple Grove, our 115-year-old family home in Hendersonville, North Carolina. Although they do require some help, especially Gladys, both these joyful ladies basically do for themselves. They didn't slow down a bit even at age 80. They zoomed through it like it wasn't there.

The most recent studies indicate people spend between 80 and 90 percent of their final working year's income in the first few years of life after work. The erroneous 60 percent figure of yesteryear wasn't in, or even close to, the ballpark. These same studies also show people emphatically do not want to reduce their lifestyles unless they're forced to.

If a young person begins his or her career around age 25, he or she will work for the next 35 to 40 years. During that period, money will have to be set aside for the 20 to 30 years of life beyond work. Social Security won't support more than a meager lifestyle at best. Fewer and fewer companies have pension plans employees don't have to contribute to. The chance of winning the lottery is one in many millions. Providing for the future is up to each individual, or else the future won't be provided for short of a substantial inheritance appearing out of the blue.

To calculate approximately how much you'll need in the future is easy. Just fill in the worksheet on page 101. You can use it over and over as your financial needs change.

For someone my age to be making $50,000 a year is not unreasonable, nor is it an outrageous amount of money. Fifty thousand dollars doesn't go nearly as far as it used to. I want to enter a comfortable life after work at age 65, which is only 15 years away. Inflation is a factor of life, and I want to take that into account. For this illustration, I assume it will increase at 4 percent per year in the future. That's higher than the rate for the last 70 years but about in line with the past 20. The higher the inflation number I plug in, the more conservative my estimate will be. Using the Rule of 72 (the inflation rate × the rate of return = 72), I divide the inflation rate, 4, into 72 and arrive at 18. At a 4 percent inflation rate, the cost of living doubles roughly every eighteen years. If I use 3 percent, the number of years is 24; at 5 percent it's 14½.

If I'm doing well on $50,000 in 1998 and have fifteen years until life after work, my cost of living will increase 0.83 times. I multiply $50,000 times 1.83 and find that in 2014 what costs $50,000 today will cost about $82,350. My

AGE	Investor Smart		Investor Not As Smart	
	IRA CONTRIBUTION	YEAR-END VALUE	IRA CONTRIBUTION	YEAR-END VALUE
19	$2,000	$ 2,240	0	0
20	2,000	4,748	0	0
21	2,000	7,559	0	0
22	2,000	10,706	0	0
23	2,000	14,230	0	0
24	2,000	18,178	0	0
25	2,000	22,599	0	0
26	2,000	27,551	0	0
27	0	30,857	$2,000	$ 2,240
28	0	34,560	2,000	4,748
29	0	38,707	2,000	7,559
30	0	43,352	2,000	10,706
35	0	76,401	2,000	33,097
40	0	134,645	2,000	72,559
45	0	237,290	2,000	142,105
50	0	418,186	2,000	264,668
55	0	736,987	2,000	480,665

	60	65		
	0	0		
	1,298,823	2,288,969	2,000	861,327
			2,000	1,532,183
Less Total Invested	(16,000)			(78,000)
Net Earnings	$2,272,969			$1,454,183
Money Grew (at 12%)	143-fold			20-fold

first year of life after work (when I'm sixty-five) I'll be spending at 90 percent of that rate, which is $74,115. Longevity runs in my genes, so I will probably live another eighteen years beyond that, at which time I'll be eighty-three. With inflation staying at 4 percent, my cost of living will double to $164,700, and since I fully expect to make it to three digits, I'll make it another eighteen years beyond that. My cost of living in the year 2050: $329,400. And don't forget, that's an annual, not a lump sum, number.

With a 4 percent inflation rate, the cost of living will slightly more than double every two decades. How many decades have you got to live? Once you make a stab at that figure, it's easy to zero in on how much the next twenty, thirty, forty, fifty, sixty, or more years will cost.

Life after work will take a lot more money than most people think, especially given they don't like to reduce their lifestyles and will probably live longer than expected. Wouldn't it be terrible to have plenty of good years left and a zest for life but no money for anything more than the bare necessities?

The simplest way to invest for life after work is to participate in your company's contributory 401(k) retirement plan or its equivalent, the 403(b), if you work for a government agency or nonprofit institution. Under the typical 401(k) arrangement, you can contribute up to 15 percent of your pretax income or $9,500 in 1997 (this amount is adjusted upward for inflation each year), whichever is lower, and invest your money in a variety of mutual funds.

More and more 401(k)s allow you to invest in individual stocks other than the stock of the company offering the plan and mutual funds. If your company or organization

HOW MUCH DOES LIFE AFTER WORK COST?

The pretax income I need in 1998 to live comfortably is	$50,000	(A)
My current age is	50	(B)
The number of years until I begin life after work is	15	(C)

I think inflation will average __4__ % (D) each year until I retire. My cost of living will double every __18__ (E) years [E = 72 divided by D and rounded].

My cost of living will double __0.83__ (F) times between 1998 and the year I retire. [F is calculated by dividing E into C.]

My income the first year of life after work will need to be G = [1 + F] × A × 90%.	$82,350	(G)
My income __18__ (E) years after I begin life after work will need to be 2G. [2G = H]	$164,700	(H)

---

allows this, you will have several legs up by following the America's Finest Companies Investment Plan. Your returns will be higher, and your operating expenses will be far lower. This could mean an extra 1 to 3 percent or more per year of additional return to you.

If your company offers only mutual funds, your choices usually range from three to fifteen or more different mutual funds, plus one other—a GIC, guaranteed investment contract.

With a 401(k) or any other retirement plan to which you make annual contributions, the amount is excluded from your gross income for federal and state income tax purposes. Let's say you earn $50,000 pretax in 1998 and invest $4,000 in our company's 401(k). Your reported gross income will be reduced to $46,000. The taxes you would have paid on the $4,000 in your 401(k) are now invested for your future. This is how Uncle Sam becomes your partner when you invest in a retirement plan. He doesn't tax you on the dollars you put into it. Neither does the state where you live. Those unpaid tax dollars work for you tax-free until you begin withdrawals (which are then taxed many years down the road).

Uncle Sam will help you another way, too. He has made it expensive to voluntarily enter your retirement plan. Short of a loan, financial hardship, and a few other special considerations, once you invest money in any retirement plan you're not allowed to get it out before age 59½ without a 10 percent penalty on the amount removed. Plus you'll have to pay taxes, too. Yes, you can move your retirement funds from one plan to another. But you cannot spend the money unless you want to pay a high price. Because Uncle Sam doesn't want you to squander your retirement funds, he becomes an excellent financial friend.

Since you're probably not going to be able to structure your own portfolio in your 401(k), let me offer some advice to help you make the most of your investment dollars. First, put every single dollar you can into a 401(k). Besides the initial tax deduction, your money grows free of taxes until you begin taking it out. This is reason enough to participate, but there's another goody that lots of 401(k) participants can enjoy—a matching contribution from their employer.

The average company chips in fifty to sixty cents for every dollar the employee sets aside, sometimes up to 6 percent of pay. In the example above, the employee earning $50,000 puts $4,000 into his 401(k) in 1998. That's 8 percent of pretax income. His employer puts in fifty cents for every dollar up to 6 percent of pretax income. Six percent is $3,000. The company adds $2,000, so the total contribution for 1996 is $6,000. Even before the employee's money is invested, he's already made a 30.0 percent return on his money ($2,000 dividend by $4,000). Where else can anyone get such a phenomenal return on his money with absolutely no risk? The employer is actually paying employees to invest, and they're saving taxes to boot.

Assuming our theoretical employee is forty, sets aside $4,000 per year (with a $2,000 company match) through age sixty five, and the money grows at 12 percent in stock funds, he'll be worth $896,003. Without the $2,000 match, his money will grow to $597,336. The employer match is worth an additional $298,667. The match adds firepower to a 401(k). It's the equivalent of adding a rocket engine to a race car.

It seems a no-brainer to invest in a 401(k) and it is, but about 40 percent of Americans who can participate don't invest anything. Sadly, they'll live to regret it. Of the 60 percent who do participate, most don't invest as much as they should and could. And most invest too conservatively. They opt for money-market funds, so-called low-risk bond funds, and GICs, which guarantee a fixed return. These alternatives barely keep ahead of inflation. Too few people

BILL STATON

have their money in stock funds, which are the only places to maximize their returns. A 1993 survey of more than two hundred California companies revealed two-thirds of 401(k) assets were in GICs and money-market funds. Stock funds were avoided because they are misperceived to be too risky.

According to a *Wall Street Journal* survey, only 8 percent of all U.S. companies with one hundred and fewer employees have retirement plans. This means more than 30 million Americans will not have retirement plans unless they set them up for themselves. If you're one of the 30 million, pay close attention. I'm going to give an overview of the most common retirement plans that are simple and inexpensive for you to set up. This isn't an exhaustive treatment of the subject. Too many other books have already done that. There are dozens at your local library with lengthy sections on the various retirement plans, and quite a few are dedicated exclusively to the subject. There's more available on retirement plans than you want to know or need to know.

The IRA—individual retirement account—has been available since 1982. Any individual, including a minor, with earned income from salary, commissions, or bonuses (interest and dividend income don't count) can set aside up to $2,000 each year in an IRA.

An IRA for a child claimed as a dependent is especially intriguing. The first $4,000 of income is sheltered by the standard deduction allowed. The next $2,000 earned can then be sheltered by the full $2,000 IRA deduction. This means a child could earn $6,000 and have no taxable income if the child fully funds his or her IRA. In addition, if this child works for a parent's proprietorship or partnership, the parent not only gets a tax deduction for the salary paid to the child, but the child (if under eighteen) is not subject to Social Security or Medicare taxes. A parent in the 50 percent tax bracket (income and self-employment income combined) would save $3,000 in taxes by putting $4,000 into the child's hands and $2,000 into the child's IRA. The result is that the IRS would pay you to save for your child's education and retirement. What a deal!

Until Congress passed tax "reform" legislation in 1986, any amount invested in an IRA was deductible from gross income. For example, if a 21-year-old in college earned $3,500 from odd jobs, the student could put as much as $2,000 of that into an IRA. Only $1,500 would be taxable. Today, money going into an IRA may be totally tax deductible, partially tax deductible, or not deductible at all. If you aren't covered by a pension plan, you can deduct every dime that goes into your IRA.

If you're married and one of you is covered by a company retirement plan, the contribution is fully deductible only if annual adjusted gross income if $40,000 or less. Singles covered by a retirement plan at work may deduct the full IRA amount if they earn $25,000 or under. Couples earning between $40,000 and $50,000 and singles earning between $25,000 and $35,000 can deduct part of their IRA contributions. Above $50,000 and $35,000 gross income, respectively, there's no deduction. But gross income can be reduced. Here's how.

Let's suppose a super-saving young couple has an adjusted gross income of $50,000 annually before plan contributions. Each has a 401(k) and participates to the limit, and each can save an additional $2,000 to go into an IRA. As a couple, they set aside the maximum 15 percent—

$7,500—into their 401(k)s. After the 401(k) contributions, their adjusted gross income is cut to $42,500. For each of the $2,000 IRA contributions, $1,500 is deductible. The other $500 isn't.

To avoid confusion, the man and woman set up two IRAs apiece—one for the money that is tax deductible; the other for money that isn't. When money begins to be withdrawn from the IRAs, which can be as early as age 59½ with no penalty imposed by the IRS, every dollar in both deductible and nondeductible IRAs is considered in a formula to determine the tax rate. It is irrelevant which IRA you take distributions from, as all amounts are aggregated. To get around this, my CPA, Paul Haisley, suggests having one spouse make the deductible contributions and the other the nondeductible contributions. Then, distributions can first be taken out of the nondeductible account to defer more of the tax.

If your situation doesn't allow you to deduct any of your IRA contributions but you can still afford to kick in $2,000 a year, I suggest doing it. The benefit to you is all the money grows with no taxes as long as the money remains in the account.

An IRA can be established at almost any financial institution—bank, savings and loan, credit union, stock brokerage. There may be a modest setup charge and what's called an annual maintenance fee in the $50–$100 range, although some firms waive all fees if the account is large enough. Since you're going to be buying shares of companies in America's Finest Companies in your IRA, you want what's called a self-directed account. This means you call the shots and decide what to buy and sell.

For the self-employed like me, there are two other retirement accounts to know about. In a sense, they are gigantic IRAs because they share many of the same features yet allow investors to sock away far more than $2,000 annually. The first is a SEP—simplified employee pension—which is almost identical to an IRA, with one huge difference. You can contribute 15 percent of your self-employment income up to a total of $30,000 per year.

As with an IRA, you can establish and contribute to a SEP for the present year as late as when you file taxes in the following year, including extensions. I don't recommend waiting that late. The earlier you make your annual contribution to a retirement plan, the harder the money will work for you. I'll show you what I mean. You have a SEP for twenty-five years and salt away $5,000 per year, which earns 13 percent in a portfolio of stocks picked from America's Finest Companies. In the first instance, you invest the $5,000 on the first business day of the year. In the second, you invest the $5,000 in the last business day of the year. By investing on the first day of the year instead of the last, you'll wind up with $879,250 rather than $778,098. That's a $101,152 increment on the same investment of $125,000 over two and a half decades. Quite a difference, isn't it?

SEPs can be opened at the same places as IRAs. So can another type of retirement plan, the Keogh. Like the SEP, a Keogh can be used if you're full-time or part-time self-employed. If you're eligible, you can contribute up to 20 percent of pretax income each year or $30,000, whichever is lower. Keoghs offer more flexibility than SEPs, and there's more paperwork involved, too. Another difference is a Keogh has to be set up by December 31 of the year in which you make the first contribution. As with a SEP, you can wait until tax-filing time to make the contribution.

Keoghs come in several types. One is the money-purchase Keogh, which allows up to 20 percent of annual self-employment income (with a $30,000 ceiling) to go into the plan. The hitch is that once you start you must put in the same percentage of income every year unless there's a loss. Skipping a contribution or falling short of the stated percentage may subject you to a huge tax penalty.

Another Keogh is the profit-sharing variety. The beauty of this plan is you can make or not make a contribution each year. You still have the $30,000 upper limit, but the percentage is lower—13 percent.

A defined-benefit Keogh allows you to salt away as much as 100 percent of your self-employment income to guarantee a certain minimum annual withdrawal once you retire. The nearer you are to life after work, the more income you can defer each year. A tax expert or actuary will need to help you if this is the route you choose to go. With the defined-benefit Keogh, you may be able to quickly "catch up" with where you need to be if you haven't planned for retirement and are in your late forties or fifties.

SEPs and Keoghs can be used for small businesses with more than one employee, and there are other retirement plans that might fit your particular needs.

One in particular is the new SIMPLE (saving incentive match plan for employees) retirement vehicle that replaces what was known as a SARSEP. I'm a founding investor–director of the new First Commerce Bank here in

Charlotte, and we've just adopted a SIMPLE plan for our employees and officers.

It can be structured like a 401(k) or an IRA, and employees may contribute as much as $6,000 (indexed annually for inflation) per year pretax. There's a mandatory (for the employer) 2 percent contribution or 100 percent match up to 3 percent of each employee's income. For a small business (in terms of the number of employees) the SIMPLE alternative is well worth checking into, especially since the complex nondiscrimination tests applied to qualified plans can be dodged.

I reiterate the advantages of all contributory retirement plans. One, the money added each year reduces your gross income, hence your current tax liability. Two, your money grows with no tax consequences until it's taken out. Three, the federal government frowns on early withdrawals, so it pays you to stick with your plan. Four, you have the tremendous opportunity to create your own mini-mutual fund of stocks culled from America's Finest Companies within your retirement plan. By doing that, your money will grow steadily at an above-average rate.

CHAPTER SEVEN

Be Your Own Money Manager

Everyone has a scheme for getting rich that will not work.

—MURPHY, ORIGINATOR OF MURPHY'S LAW

One nice thing about being your own money manager and investing exclusively in companies in America's Finest Companies is you'll only have to spend an hour or two each year (the equivalent of a long lunch) on your investment portfolio or portfolios. Then you're finished for another 365 days. It will be that easy and take that little time. This is the message I spread wherever I give a keynote address or lead a workshop. I continually butt heads against the skeptics (mostly professionals who fail to match the market indexes) who say investing can't be that easy, otherwise everyone would be doing it. But it is.

If you'll follow the steps outlined in this chapter, you can ignore daily or weekly gyrations in stock prices. In fact, you can forget about what the Dow Jones industrials, the S & P 500, or other market indexes are doing. Wouldn't that be a big relief? You can also safely ignore all forecasts about the direction of the economy and interest rates. Which way they head won't matter to you.

For the moment picture yourself as the biblical character Noah. God told you the worst storm ever was going to occur in a few months, and you needed to build a boat to withstand the coming forty-day flood. How would you have prepared for such an unprecedented event?

Noah knew. He built the craft to strict proportions to withstand the most horrible storm in history. Replicas have been tested in laboratories under hurricane conditions. Even in storms of that magnitude, the ark remained upright at all times. It never came close to capsizing.

The same principles Noah used to construct his ark are the principles you can use to guide your portfolio through economic and stock-market storms of the future. Whatever happens, you will survive and prosper because you'll know what to do, and what not to do. Your success will not be tied to how much time and effort you spend keeping up with the economy, interest rates, and the anticipated direction of stock prices.

If you love reading about business and investing, you'll probably want to continue subscribing to the publications that deal with these subjects. I suspect, though, you're heavily involved—as a parent, in your business or profession, as a community volunteer. You have little time to track stocks actively or follow the economy, and you don't want to either.

What you'll learn in this chapter will allow you to feel good about everything you're not reading. If you spend a lot of money on newspapers, magazines, and newsletters you don't want to read, cancel them. You can save hundreds of dollars every year, and the savings can go into your portfolio.

Step No 1. Be Patient

My philosophy of investing is anchored in patience. George F. Baker, founder of First National Bank of New York, the forerunner of Citicorp, said patience is one of three prerequisites for making a fortune in stocks. He knew time is on the side of the investor. He also knew that the longer anyone invests, the better his results will be. History proves it.

Since stock trading began in America in the late 1700s, the longer-term trend has been relentlessly upward. Even the Great Depression of the 1930s appears to be nothing but a blip on a two-hundred-year chart of stock prices. Naturally there are frequent, wide, day-to-day, month-to-month, and even year-to-year swings. But given enough time, stocks go only one way—UP!

Benjamin Franklin counseled, "He that can have patience can have what he will." This advice is certainly on the money for stock investors. It happens to be right for investors in every other field, too. If you'll be patient and give your stock investments time to work for you, you'll be uncommonly successful. Time (as opposed to timing) is on the side of the investor.

Perhaps the most patient investor in the world, and without question the most successful, is Warren Buffett, chairman of Berkshire-Hathaway of the New York Stock Exchange. Buffett was one of Benjamin Graham's students at Columbia University. He learned his lessons well. Berkshire-Hathaway is the most expensive stock in America and has traded for more than 48,000 per share. Buffet is one of America's wealthiest people with an estimated net worth in excess of $18 billion.

Warren Buffett has long been known for his investment prowess, but in the last few years he's been made into a virtual investment god even though he'd be first to admit that's not one of his goals. At least four books have been written about him (Buffett has never bothered to write one about himself and probably won't), and he's appeared in numerous articles in all sorts of publications. The last annual meeting of his investment company, Berkshire-Hathaway, was attended by more than seven thousand loyalists from across the globe.

What Buffett knows is well worth knowing, but I'm not sure anyone can replicate his outstanding success any more than you and I could choose to be another Michael Jordan or Picasso. It's impossible to put down on paper what makes any genius a genius, and I'm certainly not going to say I can give you the step-by-step approach to mimicking Buffett's oversize returns. I can say, however, with great certainty, that my approach is the closest thing on paper to Buffett's, so much so that I've jokingly said in my monthly *Staton Institute*^{SM} *Advisory* that Buffett reads *America's Finest Companies* when making his stock picks.

Let's look at the facts. His largest holding is Coca-Cola. He owned a large chunk of Capital Cities/ABC when it was acquired by Disney. He also owns big pieces of Gillette and McDonald's. All four are stars of America's Finest Companies. He owns a lot of American Express and, Washington Post Co., both of which have been in *America's Finest Companies*. Two of America's Finest Companies, GEICO and FlightSafety International, were both partially owned by Buffett before he bought out the rest of their stock and took them private.

If, and it's a humongous if, you'd given Buffett $10,000 to manage in 1956, it'd be well north of $100 million today. His annual rate of return has even outpaced his teacher, Benjamin Graham's, by more than six percentage points a year.

Buffett has many quotable quotes, and each is an investment lesson unto itself. "If Fed chairman Alan Greenspan were to whisper to me what his monetary policy was going to be over the next two years, it wouldn't change one thing I do."

Other Buffettisms include, "It's easier to create money than to spend it," "You have to think for yourself," "In the aggregate, people get nothing for their money from professional money managers," and "There's no use running if you're on the wrong road." Buffett believes in buying, buying more, and holding. His favorite holding period is "forever." If that's not patient, I don't know what is.

John Liscio, an astute columnist for *Barron's* (4/19/96), observed that "even in the worst of times, buying and holding stocks beat bonds all hollow. If there is any lesson that investing through the years imparts, it is that the rising tide of compound interest lifts even the most lead-footed of market timers." I found his article unusually insightful. Following a lot of research by Liscio and others, he discovered that only sixteen companies exist today that were in the original ninety companies in the Standard & Poor's market index when it began in 1926.

One thousand dollars spread equally among the ninety, with dividends reinvested, (and assuming the seventy-four companies that were in the index originally but are no longer all went bankrupt) still produced an annualized return approaching 9 percent. This works out to have produced more than ten times the amount an investor would have garnered in "ultra-safe" government bonds. Clearly patience and quality pay.

Here's another example of just how much patience pays. From time to time a bear (falling) market or sharp correction (drop) occurs and stock prices head south, sometimes violently. People without patience always panic and sell out of stocks at or near a bottom just before prices turn up. The patient investor continues to buy because he or she knows share prices are on "sale," and who among us doesn't like to buy things on sale?

The six bear markets since 1968 lasted an average of 13.5 months (range: 3–21) with an average decline of 24.4 percent (range: 14.1–42.6 percent). After they ended, the typical gain was 35.5 percent over the ensuing 12 months. Most, if not all, of the loss was quickly recouped, and stock prices then marched ahead to set new records.

Few professionals who manage other people's portfolios (I'm proud to be among this elite group) can successfully time the market and also prove that they can do it. The reason is simple. The net advance in stock prices over the long term (ten years and more) comes in brief spurts.

From 1963 through 1993 an astonishing 95 percent of the total market gain came in just 1.2 percent of total trading days. Investors have to be in to win.

I'm often asked about investing a lump sum. "Should I put it all into America's Finest Companies at once or scale in over the next few quarters?" Scaling in seems a lot safer, but it isn't. Let's say you come to me for one of my $10,000 multi-year personal coaching sessions, and you have $500,000 to invest in stocks. You're worried that the "market" is at an all-time high, which has been the case most of the time since the fall of 1990. I would respond by citing a 1994 Wright State University (Ohio) study that proves lump-sum investing is better than easing in a little bit at a time even though stock prices may appear to be overvalued. The odds would be 2-to-1 in your favor.

I would also say that trying to ease into stocks works against you psychologically. As your money coach I tell you, "Put the entire amount into stocks." You respond, "I'm scared and I'm plopping my money into a money-market fund and waiting for prices to fall. Stocks are way overpriced." Three months later the market is down 10 percent. You're right and I'm wrong. Another three months pass and stocks drop another 10 percent. You're even more right and beginning to think you know what you're doing.

Six more months zoom by and stocks this time, in what turns out to be one of the most savage bear markets since 1900, fall another 20 percent. You're still in cash and smirking. Your money coach looks like an idiot.

Suddenly and without warning stock prices stop falling and quickly turn up. Some of the companies you wanted to buy, which went on sale in the bear market, are now up

10 to 30 percent over where they were just a few weeks ago. But you don't buy. Four months later they're still climbing. You say smugly to yourself, "I'll wait for the pullback. Then I'll buy."

Four more months sail past. No pullback. Six months later, still no pullback. Stocks are soaring. All the business and stock-market news is good and getting better. Another year rushes in and out. You're still in cash. Everything you wanted to purchase is up, in most cases dramatically. Some of your choices are even ahead of where they were before they started dropping, but you refused to buy.

Pure fiction? Not exactly. In 1987 stock prices declined 40 percent (and more) in less than a month, the steepest free fall in history. The patient investor who owned America's Finest Companies was back to even in eighteen months or less and then sailed to new highs in his personal net worth.

What I recommend is easy, even with a lump sum. Pick your portfolio of at least five companies, each in a different industry, from the listing in the appendix. Invest the same dollar amount in each. Once a year when the new-edition list comes out from the author, see if the stocks you bought the previous year are still included. If they are, buy more. If one happens to have been dropped, sell and replace it with another company from America's Finest Companies.

Step No. 2. Buy More of What You Already Own

When you buy more of what you already own each year, you'll be employing the time-proven way to buy shares at reasonable prices. This technique is one you'll seldom read about in investment books. It's the only way I know to make money in any stock environment, including the Great Depression. It demands 100 percent commitment to building a diversified portfolio of quality companies. What's the way? It's dollar-cost averaging—buying the same dollar amount of common stocks over time, i.e., quarterly, semiannually, or annually. I prefer once a year because that's easy to remember and requires less record keeping.

Under dollar-cost averaging, there is absolutely no need to predict the short-term direction of stock prices. We already know the long-term direction is up. If you continue buying stocks through good and bad years, dollar-cost averaging keeps the average cost of your purchases below their average market price, guaranteeing you a profit. Here's why.

If you buy a portfolio of stocks today and their prices fall every year for the next three years (as in the Great Depression), each time you buy additional shares you'll purchase them at a lower price than before. Each time you buy more, you'll lower the average cost per share until the stocks bottom and begin to go up again. Think of buying a $400 suit. It goes on sale three months later for $300, so you buy another one in a different color because the price is so attractive. Your average cost per suit drops from $400 to $350. If you buy a third suit for $200, you'll drive the average cost down again to $300. Each suit is still worth $400, but the average cost per suit is $100 less than that.

Assuming the companies you invest in are chosen from America's Finest Companies, their stock prices will stop falling at some point and then resume their long-term uptrends. Once those uptrends begin, you'll discover your average cost per share is under the market value. You'll have a profit. On the other hand, if your stock portfolio goes up immediately and continues up, you'll have a profit, too. Either way, you'll make money. That's the extraordinary attraction of dollar-cost averaging using companies in America's Finest Companies.

Under dollar-cost averaging, it's a mathematical certainty you'll always make money as long as the companies you buy don't go out of business. If you stick exclusively with companies in America's Finest Companies, you won't have to worry about that. A company headed for serious trouble will be delisted well before it gets there.

Assume you invest $1,000 at the beginning of 1998 in a stock that doesn't pay a dividend. The cost is 10 (note:

A SIMPLE EXAMPLE OF DOLLAR-COST AVERAGING

STOCK PRICE	QUARTERLY INVESTMENT	SHARES PURCHASED	CUMULATIVE AVERAGE COST PER SHARE
10	$1,000	100.0	$10.00
9	1,000	111.1	9.47
8	1,000	125.0	8.93
7	1,000	142.9	8.35
6	1,000	166.7	7.74
5	1,000	200.0	7.09
6	1,000	166.7	6.91
7	1,000	142.9	6.92
8	1,000	125.0	7.03
9	1,000	111.1	7.19
10	1,000	100.0	7.38
Total	$11,000	1,491.4	

stock prices are written without the dollar sign) per share. You purchase 100 shares. One quarter later the stock has fallen to 9, and you spend another $1,000. The price is 10 percent lower than when you began. Instead of purchasing 100 shares, you get to buy 111.1 shares. The next quarter the price falls to 8. Then to 7, 6, and 5 in subsequent quarters. Every three months you buy $1,000 of stock.

After six installments you've invested $6,000 of your hard-earned money. The stock has collapsed 50 percent in price. Even though you are very discouraged, you continue to add to your holdings because the company is sound. You believe the stock will eventually come back.

The stock finally turns around and slowly climbs to 7. At this point, the average cost of all shares purchased is $6.92. You have a small profit. From here the profits grow larger as the stock rebounds toward the original price at which your first purchased it.

Eventually the stock recovers to 10. By now you have invested $11,000 total. The stock, first purchased for 10 per share, is still only 10. It had zero appreciation. That's the bad news.

The good news is you paid an average $7.38 for each share purchased. Your profit is $2.62 per share (excluding dividends, which would boost profits if included). The shares are valued at $14,914, a handsome return of 35.6 percent in 2½ years. And the stock is no higher than when you started.

Dollar-cost averaging worked great for an investor even during the most hostile stock-market environment in American history—the Great Depression. Nineteen twenty-nine had to be the worst time ever to start an investment program. How did dollar-cost averaging leave you if you'd been unfortunate enough to begin investing, even in the soundest of companies, on the eve of the Great Depression?

Assume you invested $1,000 on December 31, 1929. Stock prices had already crashed and begun to come down. The worst was yet to come. Standard & Poor's 500 index was 21.4. With $1,000 you would have bought 46.6 "shares" of the index. These shares produced $46 in annual dividends, which were set aside until December 31 the following year. By then the S & P had fallen 28.5 percent to 15.3. You acquired 68.2 more shares for $1,046 (your $1,000 plus the $46 in dividends).

The next December you invested another $1,000, plus $94 in dividends, and bought 134.7 shares of the S & P 500. It plunged 47.1 percent in 1931 for a dreadful 62.2 percent cumulative loss since you started just two years earlier. Time really flies when you seem to be losing money as fast as hackers lose golf balls. At the end of 1932, the market was down a whopping 67.8 percent. You had shelled out $4,265. Your portfolio was worth $2,844, a dismal 33.3 percent loss, but only half the S & P's loss.

Because you knew dollar-cost averaging demanded total devotion (at this point it seemed more like total insanity), you continued to plunk down $1,000, plus dividends, at the end of each year. By December 31, 1935, you'd invested a total of $7,995. Your gain was 27.3 percent while the S & P index was down 37.4 percent from the end of 1929. One year later you'd made a 52.7 percent profit ($14,563 divided by $9,540) while the index was still almost 20 percent under water.

Dollar-cost averaging is mechanical and overcomes one of the investor's worst enemies, his emotions. Emotions

YEAR END	REINVESTED DIVIDENDS	ANNUAL AMT. INVESTED	CUMULATIVE TOTAL INVESTED	S & P 500 12/31	TOTAL SHARES	MARKET VALUE	ANNUAL DIVIDENDS
1929	—	$1,000	$1,000	21.4	46.6	$1,000	$46
1930	$46	1,046	2,046	15.3	114.8	1,761	94
1931	94	1,094	3,140	8.1	249.5	2,026	125
1932	125	1,125	4,265	6.9	412.8	2,844	182
1933	182	1,182	5,446	10.1	529.8	5,351	238
1934	238	1,238	6,685	9.5	660.1	6,271	310
1935	310	1,310	7,995	13.4	757.7	10,176	546
1936	546	1,546	9,540	17.2	847.7	14,563	678

encourage people to buy stocks at exorbitant highs and to dump them at ruinous lows. Dollar-cost averaging puts emotion on the back burner where it belongs and gives every investor the opportunity to amass the shares of highest-quality companies—America's Finest—at reasonable (and sometimes bargain) prices. Dollar-cost averaging unfailingly produces superior results even if you have the misfortune always to buy at market peaks.

T. Rowe Price, a large mutual-fund company, proved that the commitment to invest is far more important than timing the investment. Said another way, "time in" the market is much more valuable than "timing" the market. Their study calculated the growth of a $2,000 annual IRA contribution invested in "shares" of Standard & Poor's 500 index at its highest level each year from 1969 through 1988. On July 31, 1989, the account was worth $171,757, more than four times the total investment of $40,000 spread over two decades. The compound annual total return was 10.1 percent. At that rate, money doubles every seven years, quadruples in fourteen, and expands eightfold in twenty-one.

Another study came up with a similar conclusion. If a "hypothetical hapless" investor invested $10,000 of his savings each year at the market's high from 1979 through 1994, the $160,000 total investment would have grown to more than $540,000 by the end of June 1995. That's in excess of a 235 percent gain in just a little over 16 years. A portfolio of "safe" Treasury bills invested in similar fashion (at each year's market high) grew to less than $280,000.

Smart Money magazine's September 1995 issue pointed out that during the last 25 years "the worst possible day" to have purchased stocks was January 11, 1973, one day before stock-market indexes began a 40 percent plunge over the ensuing two years. Investing in "the market" on that day, holding on for dear life, reinvesting all dividends and never adding another penny to your portfolio would have required you to wait until April 1978 just to get back to breakeven. Treasury bills and other cash equivalents would have looked much better in the short run, but in the long run they were a miserable comparison. Through mid-1995, stocks racked up a 1,022 percent gain compared to only 380 percent for cash.

Even if you wanted to, you couldn't invest at the highest point for stock prices every year for twenty straight years. You probably couldn't do it once. But even if you did, your results would still be excellent—and better than from any other investment. With America's Finest Companies, they'd be exceptional.

Step No 3. Diversify Your Holdings

How many stocks do you need in your portfolio? You can start with one, but I recommend saving enough money until you can purchase five, each in a different industry. Then you can work your way toward seven, eight, or ten, perhaps even to twelve. More than that is excessive.

Warren Buffett's Berkshire-Hathaway has major stakes in relatively few companies. He believes, as do I, that owning several dozen or several hundred companies leads to mediocrity for investors.

A number of studies show you can achieve about 90 percent of the benefits of diversification with as few as seven to eight companies, as long as each is in a different industry. The diversification table was adapted from Richard A.

	NUMBER OF STOCKS	REDUCTION IN RISK AS % OF POTENTIAL
Underdiversified	2	46.3%
	4	72.0
Well-Diversified	6	81.0
	8	85.7
	10	88.5
Overdiversified	20	94.2
	50	97.7
	100	98.8

Brealey's excellent book *An Introduction to Risk and Return from Common Stocks* (Cambridge, Mass., and London: The M.I.T. Press, 1969). Others will be somewhat different, but all reach the same conclusion.

Noted economist and successful investor John Maynard Keynes said in 1942, "I am quite incapable of having adequate knowledge of more than a very limited range of investments. To suppose that safety-first consists of having a small gamble in a large number of different directions as compared with a substantial stake in a company where one's information is adequate strikes me as a travesty of investment policy."

Keynes knew then and Buffett knows now that scattering your money into dozens and dozens of stocks (like the mutual funds do) must lead to mediocrity. *Dow Theory Forecasts* (May 26, 1997), a popular financial newsletter, concluded, "A well-constructed portfolio of 15 stocks is not significantly riskier than a 100-stock portfolio. And your chances of beating the market are much higher with a focused portfolio."

A ten-stock portfolio provides 88.5 percent of the possible advantages of diversification. Five stocks provide 77.4 percent, twenty stocks 94.2 percent. Once you own eight to ten stocks, each in a different industry, adding others reduces risk almost imperceptibly. It's hardly worth the time and effort to own lots of stocks. Warren Buffett has proved it.

Step No. 4. Buy Only Shares of Companies in America's Finest Companies

There's no special skill to making above-average profits in stocks if you (1) are patient and have an investment horizon of at least five to ten years, (2) add to your holdings regularly, (3) diversify properly, and (4) invest only in the shares of companies that will remain in business and have rising earnings and dividends. Virtually anyone, even a young person, can name at least twenty to thirty companies that fit this mold.

When my daughter was ten she picked a market-beating portfolio of eight stocks without my help. In the spring of 1988, about six months after the biggest stock crash in history, I wanted her to learn a little something about investing her own funds. She had slightly more than $4,000 cash in her college fund; the remainder was already invested.

I asked Gracie, as I fondly call her, to pick eight companies she'd like to own and purchase $500 of each through our stockbroker. It took her only a few minutes to come up with eight names. One was a private company that makes stuffed animals. Another was a yogurt chain, which neither of us knew much about. She scotched those two names and came up with two more. One was Pizza Hut, which is owned by PepsiCo. So she bought PepsiCo. She loves Coca-Cola, too, and bought $500 of that. She also loves Jeep, which is owned by Chrysler.

She was using the copier at my office, so Xerox was one stock to buy. Gracie reasoned electricity and phones will always be in vogue. She purchased Duke Energy and Bell-South. She also added McDonald's and NCNB (now NationsBank, headquartered here in Charlotte).

That's a great portfolio, don't you agree? It's high quality and well diversified, even though Coca-Cola and PepsiCo are in the same business. All eight companies are likely to survive the worst downturn in the economy any of us can imagine. How do I know that? Because all but one, McDonald's, survived the Great Depression. Even though America's Finest Companies wasn't in existence at the time, five of the eight are in it—Coca-Cola, Duke Power, McDonald's, NationsBank, and PepsiCo. Even a ten-year-old knew that you should always buy the finest companies.

There are several ways to pick a portfolio. The technique you use is not nearly as important as that you invest in nothing but the companies in America's Finest Companies. Only 3 percent of all U.S. public companies make the cut. They have the most consistent growth records. That's why they're going to make money for you regardless of how you pick the portfolio. You can bank on it because the track record is so good. On page 129 is a list of the top performing dividend payers for the past decade.

Most people will fill their portfolios with companies they've heard of. You probably will, too, and that's an excellent way to assemble your portfolio. Scan the alphabetical list of names in the appendix and circle or check the ones you like. If you need an eight-stock portfolio, you can probably find eight companies you like that are in different industries before you get into the Ds.

If you feel you need a certain amount of dividend income, your search may be limited to all the stocks yielding 4 percent or more. If you'd rather go for companies that pay little or nothing, you might choose from among the stocks yielding 1 percent or less. Maybe you like certain industries, such as banking, utilities, or consumer products. Instead of searching for companies by name, you'll scan the list in the appendix and pay close attention to the industry categories.

Another method to build your portfolio is to choose stocks randomly but not by throwing darts or drawing names. For example, you need eight stocks. Start anywhere on the list and pick every twentieth or thirtieth company until you have eight in various industries. Or pick one company from the As, Cs, Es, Gs, Is, Ks, Ms, and Os or any other group of eight letters you like. It really doesn't matter so much how you pick because you'll end up with a great portfolio in any case.

Step No. 5. Maintain the Same Dollar Amount in Each Stock

When you've chosen your portfolio of at least five companies, the next thing is to purchase approximately the same dollar amount of each. (We'll get into how to open an account and deal with a broker in chapter 10.) The first place to establish your portfolio is a retirement plan, since money will grow without tax consequences until withdrawn. For now, assume your retirement account is already open. If you're buying five companies, put 20 percent of your money into each. With eight companies,

COMPANIES WITH DIVIDEND REINVESTMENT PLANS THAT MULTIPLIED AT LEAST 7 TIMES IN VALUE IN THE PAST 10 YEARS

ONE THOUSAND DOLLARS INVESTED IN THESE THIRTY-THREE COMPANIES AT THE END OF 1986 WAS WORTH AT LEAST $7,046 BY 12/31/96, WHICH TRANSLATES INTO A MINIMUM COMPOUND ANNUAL RETURN OF 21.56 PERCENT.

COMPANY	AMOUNT
Home Depot	$29,344
Cracker Barrel Old Country	16,164
Medtronic	15,294
Gillette	14,770
Fannie Mae	13,402
Coca-Cola Co.	13,198
Wm. Wrigley Jr.	9,177
Lancaster Colony Corp.	9,037
Philip Morris Cos.	8,898
Glacier Bancorp	8,862
First Empire State Corp.	8,714
Fifth Third Bancorp	8,683
First Commercial Corp.	8,629
Franklin Resources	8,547
Schering-Plough	8,208
UST Inc.	8,203
Washington Mutual Savings	8,144
National Commerce Bancorp	8,002
Electronic Data Systems	7,940
PepsiCo Inc.	7,869
Monsanto Corp.	7,587
Century Telephone	7,538
Star Banc Corp.	7,486
Comerica Inc.	7,326
Johnson & Johnson	7,289
Nordson Corp.	7,261
Merck & Co. Inc.	7,134
AFLAC Corp.	7,092
Nucor Corp.	7,088
Procter & Gamble	7,046

12½ percent in each; with ten, 10 percent in each. Don't make the mistake so many professionals make when they try to apportion their money among the "best" companies and industries. That's speculation.

For example, a portfolio manager believes drug/health care stocks are undervalued, so he puts 25 percent of his funds into that sector. He also thinks utilities won't do nearly as well, so only 5 percent of his money goes there. When you allocate, you introduce guesswork into what otherwise is a simple process of spreading your money equally among all your holdings. Anyone can speculate about which groups and individual companies have the most promising outlooks, but that's about all they can say. They can't be sure they're going to be right until after the fact. You and I already know we can't peek into the future. I still don't understand why so many professionals believe they can.

Once you've purchased your portfolio, what's next? Nothing. You don't have to do anything until a year has passed. Let dividends accumulate in your account or automatically reinvest them (see chapter 8). On the first anniversary date of your initial purchases, put more money into your account and buy more of what you already own.

Here's an example of what to do. With $5,000 cash in your IRA, you decide to buy $1,000 of each of five companies. You'll add a sixth later. To make this example easier, I won't take commissions into account in the initial purchases. To make it more convincing, I'm using five of America's Finest Companies, each in a different industry, and going back to the first business day of 1988, January 2, so I can use real results.

The five companies I chose would all have been in

America's Finest Companies on that date. They are American Brands, a consumer-products company; Aon Corporation in insurance; Bristol-Myers Squibb, a major pharmaceutical firm; Emerson Electric, a capital-goods company; and SCANA, an electric utility.

I purposely chose five stocks that as a group appreciated far less than the market over the past five years. The odds anyone could pick five underperformers are about two out of a hundred. Odds are only one out of a hundred of choosing six. Even with this handicap, I'll demonstrate the awesome power of dollar-cost averaging and reinvesting your dividends.

It's important for you to know that I did not know in advance how this exercise was going to turn out, nor did I know what the results would be from year to year. I went through it as if I were in your shoes.

During the next twelve months, the market value of your portfolio rises 15.2 percent in value, from $5,000 to $5,760. Four stocks move higher in price, with American Brands the biggest gainer. Emerson Electric drops in price and becomes the most underweighted. At the end of 1988, here's the value of each stock ranked in descending order of value. Note each company raised its dividend during the year (a trait of stocks in America's Finest Companies), so total income is higher by 9.0 percent at year's end than at the beginning.

It's time to add another $2,000 annual contribution to your IRA. That, coupled with the $261.55 in dividends collected in the account in the first year, plus the $1 uninvested, is $2,262.55 ($2,263 rounded) for investment. Adding $2,263 to $5,760 ($8,023) and dividing by five means there should theoretically be $1,604 in each stock (again ignoring commissions). In theory, you'd buy $164 more American Brands, $400 more Aon, $479 more Bristol-Myers Squibb, $484 additional SCANA, and $734 Emerson Electric. That sounds fine on paper, but in reality it's impractical because there are commissions to consider. Most brokers charge a minimum $30 to $40 per transaction. At those rates, between $150 and $200 of the $2,263 new money to invest would be eaten up by commissions. That's too much, so I suggest a different tack.

With the $2,263, buy more of the two companies that are the most underweighted. If you used my full-service broker, you could buy thirty-five shares of SCANA for $1,120 plus roughly $40 commission ($1,160) and thirty-five Emerson Electric for $1,050 plus approximately $40 commission ($1,090). (All commissions are estimates.) There'd be $13 left in the account. The account would then look like this, with SCANA and Emerson Electric clearly overweighted, at least for now.

By the end of the second year, all five stocks have moved

JANUARY 2, 1988

COMPANY/DIVIDEND	SHARE PRICE	NUMBER SHARES	COST	ANNUAL INCOME
American Brands/$1.16	22	45	$990	$52.20
Aon Corp./$1.26	23	43	989	54.18
Bristol-Myers Squibb/$1.68	41	25	1,025	42.00
Emerson Electric/$1.03	35	29	1,015	29.87
SCANA/$2.38	28	35	980	83.30
			$4,999	$261.55
	Money uninvested		$ 1	
	Total		$5,000	

DECEMBER 31, 1988

COMPANY/DIVIDEND	SHARE PRICE	NUMBER SHARES	VALUE	ANNUAL INCOME
American Brands/$1.26	32	45	$1,440	$56.70
Aon Corp./$1.37	28	43	1,204	58.91
Bristol-Myers Squibb/$2.00	45	25	1,125	50.00
SCANA/$2.45	32	35	1,120	85.75
Emerson Electric/$1.16	30	29	870	33.64
			$5,759	
	Money uninvested		$ 1	
	Total		$5,760	$285.00

higher. Total value of the portfolio is $9,810, a 23.5 percent increase from the beginning of the year. Here's where the portfolio stands, with highest value at the top.

Since it's the beginning of year three, it's time to kick another $2,000 into your IRA and redeploy that amount, plus the $411.35 in dividends and the $13 left over from

JANUARY 2, 1989

COMPANY/DIVIDEND	SHARE PRICE	NUMBER SHARES	MARKET VALUE	ANNUAL INCOME
SCANA/$2.45	32	70	$2,240	$171.50
Emerson Electric/$1.16	30	64	1,920	74.24
American Brands/$1.26	32	45	1,440	56.70
Aon Corp./$1.37	28	43	1,204	58.91
Bristol-Myers Squibb/$2.00	45	25	1,125	50.00
			$7,929	
	Money uninvested		$ 13	
	Total		$7,942	$411.35

DECEMBER 31, 1989

COMPANY/DIVIDEND	SHARE PRICE	NUMBER SHARES	MARKET VALUE	ANNUAL INCOME
SCANA/$2.51	36	70	$2,520	$175.70
Emerson Electric/$1.28	39	64	2,496	81.92
Aon Corp./$1.49	42	43	1,806	64.07
American Brands/$1.41	35	45	1,575	63.45
Bristol-Myers Squibb/$2.12	56	25	1,400	53.00
			$9,797	
		Money uninvested	$ 13	
		Total	$9,810	$438.14

the previous year. The total market value of your stocks is $9,797. That, together with the $2,424 to reinvest, adds up to $12,228, or $2,447 per stock. SCANA and Emerson Electric are a little above that. Leave them alone. The other three are less than their proportionate weighting, with Bristol-Myers Squibb most underrepresented, followed by American Brands.

What you want to do is take the $2,424 you're adding to your portfolio and buy more shares of American Brands and Bristol-Myers Squibb. Buy twenty-one more shares of Bristol-Myers Squibb for $1,176, plus $40 commission ($1,216), and thirty-three of American Brands for $1,155 and a $40 commission ($1,195). There's $13 left over. Now the portfolio looks like the table at the top of page 135.

The portfolio has a modest gain in 1990 of 3.9 percent, but as in every year since the portfolio was begun, each of the five companies again raises its dividend. Your portfolio is now worth $12,610 with annual dividend income of $570.90, more than twice as much as when you started.

JANUARY 2, 1990

COMPANY/DIVIDEND	SHARE PRICE	NUMBER SHARES	MARKET VALUE	ANNUAL INCOME
American Brands/$1.41	35	78	$ 2,730	$109.98
Bristol-Myers Squibb/$2.12	56	46	2,576	97.52
SCANA/$2.51	36	70	2,520	175.70
Emerson Electric/$1.28	39	64	2,496	81.92
Aon Corp./$1.49	42	43	1,806	64.07
			$12,128	
		Money uninvested	$ 13	
		Total	$12,141	$529.19

DECEMBER 31, 1990

COMPANY/DIVIDEND	SHARE PRICE	NUMBER SHARES	MARKET VALUE	ANNUAL INCOME
American Brands/$1.60	41	78	$ 3,198	$124.80
Bristol-Myers Squibb/$2.40	67	46	3,082	110.40
Emerson Electric/$1.34	38	64	2,432	85.76
SCANA/$2.60	34	70	2,380	182.00
Aon Corp./$1.58	35	43	1,505	67.94
			$12,597	
		Money uninvested	$ 13	
		Total	$12,610	$570.90

At the beginning of year four, you're going to invest another $2,000 along with the $529.19 in dividends collected during the previous year and the $13 of uninvested funds, a total of $2,542. That figure added to the portfolio's $12,610 brings the total to $15,152. This means that ideally $3,030 should be invested per stock.

A quick glance at the portfolio shows American Brands and Bristol-Myers Squibb to be slightly overweighted. Emerson Electric and SCANA aren't too far off the mark, while Aon is about half what it should be. Aon needs $1,525 more to bring it up to its ideal average. The portfolio is also big enough now to add a sixth company, which is what I would suggest.

Let's assume you pick Wallace Computer Services as your sixth company. You buy forty shares of Aon for $1,400 and $40 commission ($1,440). That leaves just $1,102 to go into Wallace. You buy fifty-three shares at 20, plus $40 commission. There's just $2 left. This is the portfolio at the beginning of the fourth year:

JANUARY 2, 1991

COMPANY/DIVIDEND	SHARE PRICE	NUMBER SHARES	MARKET VALUE	ANNUAL INCOME
American Brands/$1.60	41	78	$ 3,198	$124.80
Bristol-Myers Squibb/$2.40	67	46	3,082	110.40
Emerson Electric/$1.34	38	64	2,432	85.76
SCANA/$2.60	34	70	2,380	182.00
Aon Corp./$1.58	35	83	2,905	131.14
Wallace Computer/$0.51	20	53	1,060	27.03
			$15,057	
	Money uninvested		$ 2	
	Total		$15,059	$661.13

Your fourth year investing is very satisfying as your portfolio tacks on 24.0 percent more value. Again, as in every previous year, each of your companies raises the dividend. Now it's time to make another $2,000 contribution, alongside $661 of dividends and $2 of uninvested funds—

$2,663. The portfolio is worth $18,669, so $3,555 should be apportioned to each of the six holdings ($21,330 divided by six). Bristol-Myers Squibb has the largest weighting. Emerson Electric is second and is just a few dollars off its ideal. Aon, SCANA, and American Brands aren't too wide of the mark either. Wallace Computer Services is $2,283 less than it should be.

Rather than make this complicated and to save commission, too, I'd invest the whole $2,663 in Wallace. Buy 108 shares at 24. Assuming $60 in commissions, the total spent is $2,652 with $11 remaining. How will this work out? Let's go to the end of 1992 and see.

Nineteen ninety-two wasn't a great year, since your portfolio increased less than 1 percent. Nonetheless, it was up. Wallace Computer Services and Aon Corporation scored nice gains. Emerson Electric was flat while Bristol-Myers Squibb lost 21 points, American Brands shed 5 points, and SCANA fell 4.

DECEMBER 31, 1991

COMPANY/DIVIDEND	SHARE PRICE	NUMBER SHARES	MARKET VALUE	ANNUAL INCOME
Bristol-Myers Squibb/$2.76	88	46	$ 4,048	$126.96
Emerson Electric/$1.40	55	64	3,520	89.60
American Brands/$1.81	45	78	3,510	141.18
Aon Corp./$1.66	39	83	3,237	137.78
SCANA/$2.67	44	70	3,080	186.90
Wallace Computer/$0.55	24	53	1,272	29.15
			$18,667	
		Money uninvested	$ 2	
		Total	$18,669	$711.57

JANUARY 2, 1992

COMPANY/DIVIDEND	SHARE PRICE	NUMBER SHARES	MARKET VALUE	ANNUAL INCOME
Bristol-Myers Squibb/$2.76	88	46	$ 4,048	$126.96
Wallace Computer/$0.55	24	161	3,864	88.55
Emerson Electric/$1.40	55	64	3,520	89.60
American Brands/$1.81	45	78	3,510	141.18
Aon Corp./$1.66	39	83	3,237	137.78
SCANA/$2.67	44	70	3,080	186.90
			$21,259	
		Money uninvested	$ 11	
		Total	$21,270	$770.97

DECEMBER 31, 1992

COMPANY/DIVIDEND	SHARE PRICE	NUMBER SHARES	MARKET VALUE	ANNUAL INCOME
Aon Corp./$1.77	54	83	$ 4,482	$146.91
Wallace Computer/$0.60	27	161	4,347	96.60
Emerson Electric/$1.47	55	64	3,520	94.08
American Brands/$1.97	40	78	3,120	153.66
Bristol-Myers Squibb/$2.88	67	46	3,082	132.48
SCANA/$2.73	40	70	2,800	191.10
			$21,351	
		Money uninvested	$ 11	
		Total	$21,362	$814.83

To date, you've shown the following results and a profit every year for five straight years:

1988	+15.2%
1989	+23.5
1990	+ 3.9
1991	+24.0
1992	+ 0.5

This is equivalent to a compound annual return of 13.0 percent, one percentage point better than the market's return since World War II. And remember, it was achieved with six stocks that all lagged the market, in some cases by a wide margin.

At this point you have a portfolio that's grown from $5,000 at the beginning of year one (1988) to $21,362 at the end of five years (1992). You added $2,000 per year for four years, which combined with the original capital of $5,000 is a total of $13,000 invested. The $8,362 difference (64 percent more than you put in) is from appreciation and dividends reinvested. Annual dividend income is now more than three times what it was just five years ago.

The portfolio is out of balance because Aon and Wallace Computer Services are far larger than the other four positions. You're going to add another $2,000 at the start of 1993, and along with that $771 in dividends and the $11 uninvested. That adds up to 2,782 new dollars to invest. By adding $2,782 to the portfolio's value, $21,362, we get $24,144, which works out to $4,024 per stock. You could purchase thirty-five shares of SCANA for $1,390 and $40 commission ($1,430), and nineteen Bristol-Myers Squibb for $1,273 plus $40 commission ($1,313). There'd be $29 left over.

At the beginning of 1994, you make the regular $2,000 contribution to your portfolio, which was up again for the

JANUARY 2, 1993

COMPANY/DIVIDEND	SHARE PRICE	NUMBER SHARES	MARKET VALUE	ANNUAL INCOME
Aon Corp./$1.77	54	83	$ 4,482	$146.91
Bristol-Myers Squibb/$2.88	67	65	4,355	187.20
Wallace Computer/$0.60	27	161	4,347	96.60
SCANA/$2.73	40	105	4,200	286.65
Emerson Electric/$1.47	55	64	3,520	94.08
American Brands/$1.97	40	78	3,120	153.66
			$24,024	
		Money uninvested	$ 29	
		Total	$24,053	$965.10

DECEMBER 31, 1993

COMPANY/DIVIDEND	SHARE PRICE	NUMBER SHARES	MARKET VALUE	ANNUAL INCOME
Wallace Computer/$0.64	34	161	$5,474	$103.04
SCANA/$2.74	50	105	5,250	287.70
Aon Corp./$1.80	48	83	3,984	149.40
Emerson Electric/$1.56	60	64	3,840	99.84
American Brands/$1.97	33	78	2,574	153.66
Bristol-Myers Squibb/$2.92	58	65	3,770	189.80
			$24,892	
		Money uninvested	$ 29	
		Total	$24,921	$983.80

sixth year in a row. That, coupled with $965 in dividends accumulated in 1993 and the $29 uninvested funds in your account, adds up to $2,994. Add that figure to the $24,921 portfolio value and you have $27,915—$4,653 ideally invested in each of the six companies.

The two smallest positions are Bristol-Myers Squibb and American Brands. You can buy more of each: fifty-two shares of American Brands ($1,716 and $50 commission) and twenty Bristol-Myers Squibb ($1,160 and $40 commission), a total investment of $2,966. There's $28 uninvested.

The first edition of this book ended with the portfolio below, but rather than show all the additional portfolios (which I track on my computer) since then in this newest edition, I'm going to describe the results to date. I'm certain that by now you understand how to keep adding to your portfolio and rebalance it, all the while keeping time and commissions to the bare minimum.

JANUARY 2, 1994

COMPANY/DIVIDEND	SHARE PRICE	NUMBER SHARES	MARKET VALUE	ANNUAL INCOME
Wallace Computer/$0.64	34	161	$5,474	$103.04
SCANA/$2.82	50	105	5,250	296.10
Bristol-Myers Squibb/$2.92	58	85	4,930	248.20
American Brands/$1.97	33	130	4,290	256.10
Aon Corp./$1.80	48	83	3,984	149.40
Emerson Electric/$1.56	60	64	3,840	99.84
			$27,768	
		Money uninvested	$ 28	
		Total	$27,796	$1,152.68

The portfolio dropped 3.1 percent in value in 1994 (following a meager rise of 3.6 percent in 1993), in line with the general market, from $27,796 to $26,945. During the year, Aon Corp. split its stock 3-for-2, which means that for every two shares an investor owned he received one additional share. At year's end the number of Aon shares had increased from 83 to 125.

Two thousand dollars was again invested in the portfolio on January 2, 1995, along with $1,168 in dividends collected during the previous year and a few dollars in uninvested cash. I decided to add a seventh stock in America's Finest Companies, McDonald's. I purchased 109 shares at 29 for a total cost of $3,161 plus commission. McDonald's had the lowest weighting of all seven stocks in the portfolio, but that was okay. Total value of the portfolio: $30,088.

In 1995 I had to make a sell for the first time. Wallace Computer Services was the subject of what I thought was a generous buyout offer from Moore Corp., so I sold all 161 shares on September 11 at 57¾ minus commission. (It was 29 at the start of the year.) I bought 200 shares of Loral Corp. (which was on the "Finest Buys" list in my monthly newsletter, *The Staton Institute*SM *Advisory*) and added to McDonald's—103 more shares at 37. SCANA had a 2-for-1 stock split during the year, so the number of shares doubled from 105 to 210.

By the way, 1995 was one of the best years for stocks, but this portfolio outshone all but a handful of money managers. It rose from $30,088 at the beginning of the year to $48,479 at year's end, a whopping 61.1 percent gain. That was so spectacular even I had a hard time believing it, but it was true.

Through the end of 1995, the portfolio's annual returns look like this:

1988	+ 15.2%
1989	+ 23.5
1990	+ 3.9
1991	+ 24.0
1992	+ 0.5
1993	+ 3.6
1994	− 3.1
1995	+ 61.1
1996	+ 23.8

Excluding annual contributions, the compound annual return for the nine years to date is 15.7 percent per year, in line with the 13–15 percent historic performance of the companies in America's Finest Companies. Again, I'd like to reemphasize that I've stacked this IRA portfolio with companies (excluding McDonald's and Loral Corp.) that have been performing worse than stocks in general. The odds of doing that accidentally are less than one in one hundred.

As always, I added another $2,000 on January 2, 1996 to the IRA and used that, along with $1,169 in dividends and $22 uninvested cash, to purchase Emerson Electric, the most underweighted stock at the end of 1995. I bought 38 shares at 82, and that kicked the number of shares from 64 to 102. The chart on page 144 shows what the portfolio looked like ranked in order of value.

Stocks came out of the starting gate with a bang in 1996 and by January 8 another company in the IRA was bid for. Lockheed Martin (in America's Finest Companies) said it

BILL STATON

JANUARY 2, 1996

COMPANY/DIVIDEND	SHARE PRICE	NUMBER SHARES	MARKET VALUE	ANNUAL INCOME
McDonald's Corp./$0.27	45	212	$ 9,540	$ 57.24
Emerson Electric/$1.96	82	102	8,364	199.92
Bristol-Myers Squibb/$2.96	86	85	7,310	251.60
Loral Corp./$0.32	35	200	7,000	64.00
Aon Corp./$1.36	50	125	6,250	170.00
SCANA/$1.44	29	210	6,090	302.40
American Brands/$2.00	45	130	5,850	260.00
			$50,404	
		Money uninvested	$ 50	
		Total	$50,454	$1,305.16

wanted to acquire Loral Corp. I sold Loral at 44½ minus commission and bought 300 John H. Harland at 21 and 170 Washington REIT at 15, both plus commission. Both Harland and Washington were on my "Finest Buys" list on that date. Both had been relative underperformers for several years, but I thought the value was there. Certainly there appeared to be little, if any, downside risk because the dividend yields from both were so far above that of the typical stock.

Nineteen ninety-six was another terrific year for stocks as the major stock-market indexes soared to new all-time highs. I sold all 300 shares of John H. Harland on December 6 when the company failed to raise its dividend (thus being eliminated from America's Finest Companies) and purchased 430 more shares of Washington REIT at 16, plus a small position in 100 shares of Parker Hannifin at 41.

144

JANUARY 8, 1996

COMPANY/DIVIDEND	SHARE PRICE	NUMBER SHARES	MARKET VALUE	ANNUAL INCOME
McDonald's Corp./$0.27	45	212	$ 9,540	$ 57.24
Emerson Electric/$1.96	81	102	8,262	199.92
Bristol-Myers Squibb/$2.96	84	85	7,140	251.60
Aon Corp./$1.36	51	125	6,375	170.00
John H. Harland/$1.02	21	300	6,300	306.00
SCANA/$1.44	28	210	5,880	302.40
American Brands/$2.00	45	130	5,850	260.00
Washington REIT/$1.00	15	170	2,550	170.00
			$51,897	
Money uninvested			$ 25	
Total			$51,922	$1,717.16

By year's end the portfolio had garnered a 23.8 percent total return, making the record to that date look like this:

1988	+15.2%
1989	+23.5
1990	+ 3.9
1991	+24.0
1992	+ 0.5
1993	+ 3.6
1994	− 3.1
1995	+61.1
1996	+23.8

On January 2, 1997, I again (as I have done each year) added another $2,000 IRA contribution and the $7 in the account that was uninvested. I purchased 50 more shares of Parker Hannifin at 39 for $1,950 plus $40 commission, a total of $1,990, leaving $17 uninvested. Market value of the portfolio on that date was $65,269.

I made some other buys and sells in the next few months and on June 2, 1997, decided to add a new section to my newsletter called *Bill Staton's 3 Guided Portfolios.* I had been using the portfolio from this book in my advisory, so at that time I dropped it in favor of the three new ones. The eight stocks in the portfolio were Parker Hannifin, McDonald's, Washington REIT, Emerson Electric, Aon Corp., Duke Energy, Block Drug, and AMP. The Dow Jones industrial average was 7331. The portfolio was worth $72,680, for a gain of 11.4 percent in five months. All but Emerson and Aon are in one of the guided portfolios.

Although there's no practical way to keep exactly one eighth of your portfolio in each of the eight companies, you've done an excellent job so far by buying more shares each year of the one or two most underweighted companies in the portfolio. You're getting more than 85 percent of the benefits of diversification with just eight companies. With occasional juggling, you can keep your portfolio in good proportion while still adding the annual $2,000 maximum and reinvesting all dividends and uninvested cash. The balance doesn't have to be perfect, only as exact as you can make it.

STEP NO. 6. SELL RARELY

To recap: Start with a portfolio of at least five stocks in America's Finest Companies. Each year check the latest compilation of America's Finest Companies to see whether all the companies you own are still included. If they are, buy more as shown above. If one's been knocked out of the box, replace it with another. By using this simple approach, you'll sell infrequently while simultaneously continuing to accumulate shares of the finest companies on the market.

Stock-market and investing books are chock-full of all sorts of information, much of it half-baked, about how to time the market and sell at the right times. I'm not very good at selling because it's much more difficult to know when a stock is overpriced than it is to know when it's underpriced. Spotting a cheap stock and buying it is easy for me. Finding one that's not going any higher and may be headed for a fall is a lot tougher.

That's why I recommend only two reasons to sell. One is to get rid of a stock that's been dropped from America's Finest Companies. You sell all of it. Two is you need the money. You may sell part or all of your holdings depending on how much money is required. Other than these, I recommend buying and not selling.

I'm in the camp with Warren Buffett. Buffett says he loves buying, but selling is a different story. He compares the pace of his selling activity with a traveler stranded in Podunk's lone hotel. There was no TV in the room, so the stranger faced a long unfruitful evening. However, he soon discovered a book on his night table called *Things to Do in Podunk.* Excitedly opening it, the traveler found only a single line, "You're doing it."

You can be your own successful money manager by following these six steps:

1. Be patient
2. Buy more of what you already own
3. Diversify your holdings
4. Buy only the shares of companies in America's Finest Companies
5. Maintain the same dollar amount in each stock
6. Sell rarely

Of course you can make managing your money a lot more complicated than this. Most professionals and ordinary folk do. But it's not necessary. Why make money the hard way if there's an easier way? That's what I've always asked myself. By the time I was thirty-one, I had earned my first million from investing in stocks. I spent a lot of time analyzing and agonizing over my portfolios. Within five years, I was worth more than three million. Getting to that point was a lot easier because I was simplifying the process. Today my personal investment process, the one I recommend for all my clients, is the same one I'm advocating for you. It's easy to understand, simple to put into practice, and most important, it works.

Opponents of my method will mention this or that mutual fund that has, according to some mutual-fund survey, beat the pants off the market in recent years. They'll wonder why you weren't investing in those funds. Good question. In chapter 5, I proved most funds fail even to equal the market every year, let alone beat it. The percentage of stock funds that will beat the market over any ten-year period is remarkably small—less than 5 percent from 1983 to 1993. Will you be able to pick the market beaters from more than nine thousand funds? I'll give odds you won't, and I'll win more than enough bets to retire wealthy from the bets alone.

Stocks in America's Finest Companies, as a group, have consistently beaten the market by several percentage points, either from capital appreciation alone or with dividends reinvested. The stocks from "The Super 50 Team" with dividend reinvestment plans returned 17.6 percent compounded annual versus 15.6 percent from the S & P 500. That's a 2.0 percent difference. Suppose five of those stocks were your portfolio over the past decade and commissions were a whopping 10 percent on each $2,000 investment as well as on the initial $5,000. The first $4,500 ($5,000 less $500 commission) investment would have grown to $35,377. The remaining nine $1,800 annual contributions ($2,000 less $200 commission) would have piled up to $52,135, a total of $87,512. That same money invested in the market, assuming no loads or annual fees, would have amounted to $63,503, or $24,009 less.

GETTING STARTED WITH A LITTLE
OR A LOT

I've shown you how to start with $5,000 and add $2,000 a year, the maximum allowed by law, to an IRA. But you may have a lot less than that to begin with, or you may have a lot more.

Suppose you're eighteen and in college. You get a job as I did when I was in school and earn $2,500 each of the four years you're there. You need most of that money for living expenses but can invest $50 each month. Since you have earned income, you're allowed to contribute to an IRA.

You open an account with a discount brokerage firm (where commissions are cheaper) and mail them a $50 check monthly for twelve months; this is invested in a money-market fund earning 3 percent. At the end of the year you've saved $600 and earned about $9 interest. Pick one stock you like from the stocks in America's Finest Companies and buy it. Less $35 estimated commission (because you're using a discount broker) you'll put roughly $574 to work. Follow the same routine each of the next three years you're in school and buy a different stock each time. Make sure it's in a different industry.

When you graduate, you'll have invested $2,400 (less commission) and will own a few shares of four different companies. Since you're armed with a college degree, you should soon start earning far more than $2,500 and be able to contribute the maximum $2,000 per year if your employer doesn't offer a 401(k) plan. If your employer does, you should invest in his plan first because you can put away far more than $2,000 per year. For this example, I'm assuming you're not covered at work.

You're now twenty-two and your little IRA has grown to $4,000. No doubt it's out of balance. When you make your first $2,000 annual contribution, you'll have enough money to add a fifth stock in a different industry. Follow the same technique outlined earlier to invest $2,000 annually and maintain balance. Sounds simple, and it is.

Now let's shift gears for a minute and pretend you're self-employed. No one else works for you. You realize you've got zero dollars set aside for life after work and need help, so you rush out and purchase a copy of this book. After completing chapter 6 on retirement plans, you open an SEP or Keogh. Take your pick. You fund it with a

$10,000 contribution at age 50 and bump up the contribution each year by 10 percent. By age 60, you're up to $25,937 annually, which is $4,063 less than the maximum $30,000 you're allowed to contribute under today's law. By the time you're 60 the limit is probably going to be significantly higher. Your money grows at 12 percent each year, the same rate as common stocks since World War II. Since you're investing exclusively in America's Finest Companies, it ought to grow at 13–15 percent, but I'm being conservative.

You see from this example that after eleven annual contributions (at the beginning of each year), you've put $185,310 into your SEP or Keogh. When you are age 65,

A SEP/KEOGH GROWS RAPIDLY EVEN WHEN YOU START LATE

START AGE	ANNUAL $ CONTRIBUTION INCREASES 10% ANNUALLY/EARNS 12% TAX DEFERRED
50	10,000
51	11,000
52	12,100
53	13,310
54	14,641
55	16,105
56	17,716
57	19,487
58	21,436
59	23,579
60	25,937

Total Contributions: $185,310
Worth at Age 65: $551,112
Worth at Age 70: $971,248
Worth at Age 75: $1,711,671

it will have grown to $551,112 (nearly tripled) and five years later will be approaching a million dollars (more than quintupled).

If you can start a portfolio with as much as $10,000 and add at a rate similar to this, you should spread the money equally among six companies rather than five. In the illustration you could stay with six stocks until age 55 and then add a seventh, which ought to be sufficient diversification. Again, you'll follow the same technique described earlier.

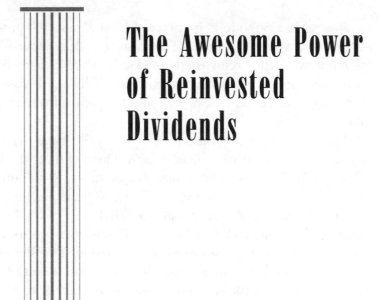

CHAPTER EIGHT

The Awesome Power of Reinvested Dividends

Whenever you see the compound annual returns from the Dow Jones industrial average and Standard & Poor's 500 composite index, they include quarterly reinvestment of all dividends. Without dividend reinvestment, annual returns from stocks would be about as exciting as watching a silent movie.

One dollar invested in the S & P 500 at the end of 1925, with dividends reinvested, mushroomed to $1,113.92 by the end of 1995. John Connallon, an investment strategist at Smith Barney, asked a number of the firm's research analysts to guess what percentage was from capital appreciation and what was from dividend reinvestment. The

average guess came in at 60 percent capital gains, 40 percent dividend reinvestment. The answer is that about 95
percent was from reinvested dividends while 5 percent
was from capital gains. Said another way, dividends reinvested generated nearly twenty times the return from capital appreciation.

Approximately one thousand companies allow you to automatically reinvest your dividends in shares of their stock
through DRPs—dividend reinvestment plans. Two hundred ninety-four of America's Finest Companies have
them. The standard way to open a DRP is to buy a few
shares of a company (like Hershey Foods) that offers it
and have the shares registered in your name. The shares
are then mailed directly to you, along with a simple DRP
signup form. You fill in a few blanks and return it to the
company. Each quarter, instead of mailing you a dividend
check, Hershey and every company in whose DRP you
participate will send you a form like the one shown on the
following page.

All DRP statements are similar and easy to read. This
one is the statement of my eight-year-old son, Will, who
owns more than four hundred shares of this particular
company. He also participates in four other DRPs. You
probably already guessed the companies are among America's Finest Companies. Since he's a minor, an adult has to
be custodian of the account. In this case Will's mother is
his custodian.

The bottom left-hand corner of this statement shows
that 412 shares are owned by Will and registered in his
name outside the plan. Just to the right of that number,
you see 25.7178. That's the number of shares Will had in
the plan before the most recent dividend was reinvested.

DIVIDEND REINVESTMENT AND STOCK PURCHASE PLAN

Public Service Company
Of North Carolina Inc

SHAREHOLDER
ACCOUNT NUMBER
XXXX

TAXPAYER IDENTIFICATION
NUMBER

FOR SHAREHOLDERS OF PUBLIC SERVICE COMPANY OF NORTH CAROLINA, INC.   **XXX-XX-XXXX**

ADDRESS ALL CORRESPONDENCE TO

FIRST UNION NATIONAL BANK, AGENT
DIVIDEND REINVESTMENT SERVICE
TWO FIRST UNION CENTER
CHARLOTTE, N.C. 28288 1154
(1-800-829-8432)

JOHN DOE
1111 MAIN STREET
CHARLOTTE NC 11111   AMOUNT ENCLOSED:

TO MAKE AN OPTIONAL CASH PAYMENT, PLEASE DETACH AND MAIL WITH YOUR CHECK

FOR SHAREHOLDERS OF PUBLIC SERVICE COMPANY OF NORTH CAROLINA, INC.

Shareholder Account Number:	Taxpayer Identification Number	Investment Date	Record Date		Dividend Payment Date	Quarterly Dividend Rate Per Share
XXXXX	XXX-XX-XXXX	10/01/93	09/10/93		10/01/93	$.19750

DATE OF TRANSACTION	TYPE OF TRANSACTION	AMOUNT OF TRANSACTION	SERVICE CHARGE	NET AMOUNT INVESTED	PRICE PER SHARE	SHARES ACQUIRED OR WITHDRAWN	TOTAL SHARES HELD IN PLAN
					PRIOR BALANCE ♦♦♦♦♦♦ ►		10.1880
01/04/93	STOCK DIVIDEND	0.00	.00	0.00	0.0000	5.0940	15.2820
04/01/93	COMMON DIVIDEND	78.28	.00	78.28	16.2450	4.8187	20.1007
04/01/93	PLAN DIVIDEND	2.90	.00	2.90	16.2450	0.1785	20.2792
07/01/93	COMMON DIVIDEND	81.37	.00	81.37	15.6988	5.1832	25.4624
07/01/93	PLAN DIVIDEND	4.01	.00	4.01	15.6988	0.2554	25.7178
10/01/93	COMMON DIVIDEND	81.37	.00	81.37	17.5038	4.6487	30.3665
10/01/93	PLAN DIVIDEND	5.08	.00	5.08	17.5038	0.2902	30.6567

PLAN DATA FOR CURRENT PERIOD

FIVE-DAY AVERAGE CLOSING PRICE	PURCHASE PRICE WITH REINVESTED DIVIDENDS	WITH OPTIONAL CASH PAYMENTS	AVERAGE OR HIGH AND LOW PRICE ON				
			10/01/93				
18.425	17.5038	18.425	17.875				

Shares held on record date HELD BY YOU	HELD IN PLAN		TOTAL DIVIDENDS PAID	TAX WITHHELD IF ANY	NET DIVIDEND REINVESTED	SERVICE CHARGES	SHARES ACQUIRED WITH REINVESTED DIVIDENDS AND OPTIONAL CASH	TAXABLE DIVIDEND INCOME
FULL	FULL	Fraction						
412	25.7178	Current	86.45	0.00	86.45	0.00	4.9389	88.29
		Year to Date	333.37	0.00	333.37	0.00		349.14

(See the reverse side for additional information)
IMPORTANT: RETAIN THIS STATEMENT FOR YOUR INVESTMENT AND TAX RECORDS

FORM P503 (10.93)

155

This is the last of four statements Will received in 1993. On October 1 a total of $86.45 in dividends was used to purchase more stock; $81.37 was from the 412 shares outside the plan, $5.08 from the shares inside the plan. There was no service charge to buy the new shares, so 100 percent of the dividend went to work for Will. The price per share was 17.5038, and 4.9407 shares were acquired (4.6987 plus 0.2902). After the dividends were reinvested, Will owned 30.6567 shares within the DRP.

This company will automatically reinvest dividends each quarter, and there are no commissions or other charges. The company absorbs them for you. That's one great benefit of participating in DRPs. Many companies pick up the entire commission tab. Even if they don't, using a DRP is still a good deal because the commissions (and other charges) are far less than you'd pay a broker, especially on a small amount of money like $86 per quarter.

Most companies with DRPs also offer OCPs—optional cash payment plans. The company in this example does, too. About one-third down from the top of the form note the sentence "To make an optional cash payment, please detach and mail with your check." You tear off the top of the form and send it in with your money. OCPs have minimum and maximum amounts that can be contributed each quarter. The minimum is typically $25–$50 while the maximum can be $1,000, $2,000, and sometimes unlimited.

Each quarter when this statement comes in, we have the option (but we don't have to exercise it) to mail as little as $25 or as much as $3,000 to the address shown and buy more shares of stock for Will. As with reinvested dividends, this company also pays the commission. If we send in $1,000 the entire $1,000 goes to work for my son, not a broker. If we buy more shares through the lowest-cost broker we can find, we're looking at $25 or more in unnecessary commissions.

Because of DRPs and OCPs, it's possible to begin a portfolio with $500 or less and still invest in five different companies. The technique I'm discussing here is especially useful for a young person or anyone else who can only afford to start small. Let's assume twenty-year-old Mary saves $50 a month for ten months to accumulate $500. She picks five companies with dividend reinvestment plans, each in a different industry. For simplicity, let's also assume each company sells for $50 per share and the commission to buy one share is also $50. Mary plunks down $500, $250 of which buys five shares of stock. The other $250, half her money, goes to the broker. This is not a good deal for Mary if she keeps investing $500 at a time because the broker will be taking half. But it is when she utilizes the OCPs.

Mary makes sure the one share of each of the five companies is registered in her name (not in "street" name, meaning it is held by the broker) and delivered to her. She then signs on for each company's dividend reinvestment plan. After the companies pay their next quarterly dividends, Mary will receive five statements that look similar to Will's statement. Almost without question, all her companies will have optional cash payment plans, and those will show on the fronts of the statements.

Before making her initial purchases, Mary should call each company (phone numbers are in the appendix) and ask for DRP and OCP information. She'll want to know about service fees and commissions, if any, and minimum-maximum limits for the OCPs. More and more companies offering DRPs charge a service fee. In most cases, they're capped and are little more than a nuisance. As the number of shares owned grows larger, the service fee shrinks as a percent of the dividends reinvested. Even so, if you're working with a small amount of money, the charges from some companies might make quarterly reinvestment a bad deal.

Mary will also want to inquire whether buying one share of stock is enough to open a company's DRP. If not, there are plenty that only require one share to begin. Those are the companies to stick with.

For years, one of the companies in America's Finest Companies, Bristol-Myers Squibb, would allow investors to begin a DRP with just one share of stock. They could also buy additional shares with their cash dividends without paying a fee or brokerage commission. Stock purchases up to $3,000 per quarter were also free of fees or commissions. Then the company had a change of heart. It set a fifty-share minimum to participate in the DRP and also initiated a charge on shares purchased through the plan, and another charge when the shares are sold.

Mary continues to save $50 per month. After two months she has $100 to be mailed to the first of the five companies for investment. After two more months, she mails another $100 to the second, and so forth. At the end of twelve months, $600 is invested—$200 in the first company and $100 apiece in companies two through five. The next $100 goes into the second company, and the cycle continues.

After two years, the portfolio will be out of balance because one or more of the stocks will have done better than the others. That's easy to correct. Mary adjusts her optional cash payments to buy a little more of the stocks that have gone up the least and a little less of the ones that have gone up the most. As she gradually increases her savings from $50 to $60 to $70 and more per month, she increases the size of the extra cash payments. All the while she's paying no commission dollars to a broker. Her companies are picking up all, or most, of the transactions costs. As Mary continues her dollar-cost averaging program through the years, she'll save hundreds, if not thousands, in commissions. All those saved dollars will be working for her.

When I started an investment program for Will in 1992, his mother and I invested roughly $5,000 in each of five different companies. Total commissions were $621 through our full-service broker. As we invest an additional $5,000 per company, we'll save the entire $621 because Will's companies will absorb the costs. Since Will is only eight, the $621 we don't spend—and which should compound at 13–15 percent annually—will grow to a minimum of $950,163 and a maximum of $2,722,463 by the time Will is 65. Staggering, isn't it?

There are drawbacks to dividend reinvestment plans whether they have the optional cash-payment feature or not. One is you can't instantly sell the shares held in the plan. You have to detach part of the quarterly DRP form and mail it back to the company or the financial institution administering the plan. With one of Will's companies, you'd have three options: (1) a stock certificate in your name for some of the shares in the plan (you name the amount); (2) a stock certificate in your name for all shares in the plan and your participation terminated; (3) your plan participation terminated by selling all and partial shares at the next available date, then the proceeds mailed to you. If the shares were in a brokerage account, you could sell them and get the money in a few days, sometimes the same day. With a DRP it will take weeks.

I own shares in a DRP that won't sell them for me. They'll mail me a certificate for all or some of the shares if I ask. Then I have to take the certificate to my broker to sell them. All that takes time and effort on my part.

When you want to buy shares of a company, you simply call your broker and buy them. In an OCP it can take weeks for the company to invest your money. Why? Because the company pools everyone's OCP contributions and buys only at certain times of the year. Your money and everyone else's sits idle in an omnibus account without earning interest until investment day arrives. That's bad. What's good is buying in "bulk" allows a company to keep commission expenses minimal.

Another drawback to a DRP is you need to save the final quarterly statement of each company each year for tax purposes. It will show all four quarterly transactions and the amounts of dividends reinvested. Otherwise you won't know how much you paid for the shares. One trap a lot of investors fall into is they pay taxes twice on reinvested dividends. First, they pay taxes on dividends in the year they were reinvested. If they fail to add those reinvested dividends back to the cost of the original shares and "step up" their cost basis, they'll pay taxes on the dividends again when the shares are sold because the capital gain will be larger than it should be.

If you participate in a lot of DRPs, as some investors do, you'll never have an accurate picture of the value or balance of your portfolio unless you calculate it. And you might not be able to use DRPs for your retirement plan. That's because a financial institution has to domicile the account and hold all your securities in street name. When they're in street name, you can't participate in DRPs.

It is possible to participate in individual company dividend reinvestment plans through retirement plans, but it's not for everybody. A lot depends on the current size of your account because the fees involved might end up being more than the commissions you save.

There are several financial institutions across the country that handle this unusual service, and the leader appears to be First Trust. You can call them at 800/863-2608 for more information and a free kit, or visit their web site at www.firsttrust.com. First Trust advertises that "if you are looking for a way to save with minimal investment amounts, the DRP IRA is for you." They also say that if you have rollovers, transfers, SEPs, or account consolidations worth $100,000 and more, they offer a free jumbo IRA.

First Trust has no establishment fees, no commissions or transaction fees, and a minimal annual fee for smaller accounts. For the jumbos, the annual fee is waived. If you try First Trust and like them, please let me know.

For investors seeking dividend reinvestment without having to open accounts with each company, a number of brokerage firms, both large and small, have come to the rescue and more are on the way. Firms including Charles Schwab, Smith Barney, and Merrill Lynch allow investors to participate in the DRPs of approximately four thousand companies, whether those companies have DRPs in place or not. One terrific benefit is that retirement plans are usually included. Schwab is the nation's largest discount broker, whereas Merrill Lynch is the largest full-service firm. Smith Barney is one of the larger full-service firms as well.

There are many advantages to reinvesting dividends through a brokerage account rather than company by company. First, you can add the awesome power of dividend reinvestment for your retirement plan as well as for a taxable account. Second, you'll get one monthly statement (rather than quarterly statements from individual companies) showing the value of each stock and the amount of dividends reinvested. It's much easier to keep your portfolio balanced when all your holdings are together. It's easier at tax time, too, because all transactions are on one statement, not several.

Third, if you happen to lose one of your brokerage statements, it's easy to get a replacement by calling your account executive. I can get a copy from my broker by fax the same day I request it. If you lose a company's DRP statement, it's sometimes difficult to get another copy. More than one phone call or letter may be required.

Fourth, there are so many more companies from which to choose. I don't know the exact number of companies offering DRPs, but there are estimates ranging from nine hundred to eleven hundred. I usually say about a thousand. By going through a broker for dividend reinvestment, you can choose from close to four thousand companies.

Since I want you to invest only in America's Finest Companies, having four thousand choices compared with one thousand isn't the optimum benefit. The optimum is you can reinvest quarterly dividends in virtually all the companies in America's Finest Companies in either a taxable account, a nontaxable account, or even better, both. There's an easy way to find out which qualify; just ask the broker before making your purchases. If one you like isn't in their group of four thousand or so, substitute another that is. Then tell the broker you think it should be.

The main disadvantage of a dividend reinvestment brokerage account is you can't participate in optional cash payment plans. You'll always have to pay a commission to add to your holdings. To me that isn't a great detriment, but it may be to you. Is the convenience and ease of record keeping worth more than the commission costs? Only you can decide.

One way to handle this dilemma is to make taxable investments through individual dividend reinvestment plans and use OCPs to save commissions. Make nontaxable investments through a broker offering dividend reinvestment for retirement plans. Even though you won't get the benefit of OCPs, you will be able to reinvest dividends and add compounding power to your portfolio.

Earlier in the chapter I mentioned that sixteen AFC companies allow you to reinvest dividends and make optional cash payments at discounts to market value ranging from 1 percent to 5 percent. The discounts are taxable as ordinary income. The sixteen are shown here alphabetically with their discounts.

BB&T Corp.	3%
CNB Bancshares Inc.	3
Colonial Gas Co.	5
First of America Bank	5
First Union Corp.	1
H.B. Fuller Corp.	3

Household International	2.5
Mercantile Bankshares	5
New Plan Realty Trust	5
North Carolina Natural Gas	5
Old National Bancorp	3
Piedmont Natural Gas Co.	5
Telephone & Data Systems	5
United Dominion Realty	5
UtiliCorp United Inc.	5
York Financial	10

Forty-one companies in America's Finest Companies allow you to buy initial shares direct without going through a broker. They have varying requirements about the number of shares you must buy to start your investment program. Some require that you be either a customer or a resident in their service areas before making your first purchase. For specifics contact the ones in which you're interested. Their phone numbers are in the alphabetical list at the back of this directory.

AFLAC Inc.
Air Products & Chemicals
American Water Works Co.
Ameritech Corp.
C.R. Bard Inc.
Bob Evans Farms Inc.
Brooklyn Union Gas Co.
Central & South West Corp.
Connecticut Water Service
Energen Corp.
Enova Corp.

Exxon Corp.
First Commercial Corp.
Florida Progress Corp.
Gillette
Hawaiian Electric
    Industries
Hillenbrand Industries
Home Depot Inc.
Madison Gas & Electric
    Co.
McDonald's Corp.

Merck & Co. Inc.
Minnesota Power & Light
Northern States Power Co.
Old National Bancorp
Piedmont Natural Gas Co.
Procter & Gamble Co.
Public Service Co of NC
Questar
Reader's Digest Association
Regions Financial Corp.
SCANA Corp.

Union Electric Co.
UtiliCorp United Inc.
Wal-Mart Stores Inc.
Warner Lambert Inc.
Weingarten Realty
  Investors
Western Resources Inc.
WICOR Inc.
Wisconsin Energy Corp.
York International

Seven companies offer IRAs: Ameritech, Bell Atlantic, Connecticut Water Service, Exxon Corp., McDonald's Corp., SBC Communications, and UtiliCorp United.

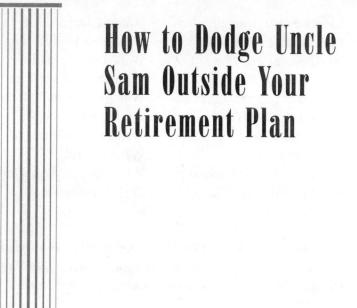

CHAPTER NINE

How to Dodge Uncle Sam Outside Your Retirement Plan

You've got to hand it to the IRS. If you don't, they'll come get it.

—ANONYMOUS

Money inside a retirement plan receives preferential treatment because it grows without taxes until withdrawn. If you sell appreciated stock in your retirement plan, there will never be any capital-gains taxes to pay. Taxes are paid only when money is withdrawn, beginning as early as fifty-nine and a half and no later than seventy and a half.

Money outside a retirement plan is treated poorly by both Uncle Sam and all the states with income taxes. Taxes on dividends and capital gains must be paid in the years they're realized. Although losses can be used to offset gains, that's not much of a benefit, because taxes can knock an iceberg-size hole in your financial ship.

Capital-gains taxes can take a huge chunk out of profits in a taxable account. That's why it makes the most sense to lock away every investment dollar possible in a retirement plan. For one thing, the government makes it hard to get money out of a retirement plan without triggering a 10 percent penalty. If you're building a stock portfolio for something other than life after work, you'll probably do it in a taxable account. Then you can get your hands on your money penalty-free anytime you want to.

To minimize taxes, you have to build a portfolio of low- to no-yielding (2 percent down to 0 percent) stocks and sell rarely. Selling rarely (and therefore not paying capital-gains taxes) is what has allowed many self-made millionaires and billionaires, members of the Forbes 400, to establish such incredible fortunes—Warren Buffett of Berkshire-Hathaway, Leon Levine of Family Dollar Stores, Leslie Wexner of The Limited, to name three.

Five years ago an attorney client, who's very well to do, flew down from Baltimore for one of my personal-coaching sessions. He already had a substantial buildup in his retirement plan and was making the maximum annual contribution each year, but he still could put a lot of extra money into his taxable portfolio. The portfolio contained a lot of low-quality stocks sprinkled with companies in America's Finest Companies, like Merck. There were capital gains in some issues, losses in the others, and no particular rhyme or reason as to what would be purchased and sold. In addition, there were far too many stocks to keep up with. My recommendation was to sell most of the stocks, offset the gains with the losses, and assemble a portfolio of ten companies in America's Finest Companies, with 10 percent of the money in each. The client and I together chose the portfolio, and the end result was one we felt comfortable with.

Without revealing what he bought, I'll show you the thought process that went into picking the ten names. You may or may not be, but my client is in a high tax bracket. With state and federal taxes combined, dividend income is taxed at approximately 45 percent. Because the combined rate is so high, it will pay my client to focus on low- or no-yielding stocks and strive for capital gains rather than dividend income. If you want to invest in stocks for a combination of yields and capital gains (utilities, for example), those stocks should be in your retirement plan, where dividends won't be taxed. When you invest outside the retirement plan, the focus should be on capital application at the expense of the yield.

A general rule of thumb is that companies whose stocks have low yields (McDonald's) or no yields (Microsoft) grow faster than their counterparts with higher yields. This is not inviolate when applied to individual companies, but for our purposes it's a good guideline when applied to companies on the whole. The reason it works is faster-growing companies figure they can earn more for shareowners by plowing earnings back into the businesses rather than paying it in dividends. Said another way, faster-growing companies earn higher returns on reinvested dollars than the typical company or investor.

Slower-growing industries like banking and utilities provide above-average dividend yields because their growth prospects aren't nearly so bright as for a Wal-Mart or a Nucor.

The twenty-five top-performing stocks in America's Finest Companies over the past ten years (from capital appreciation) were, as a group, very low-yielding stocks. Several paid no dividends at all. The rest had minuscule dividend yields. Since capital gains is what we're looking for in a taxable portfolio, below-average-yielding stocks must make up the portfolio.

It's easy to pick such a portfolio and takes no more than a couple of minutes. Turn to the alphabetical listing of companies in the appendix and start skimming the list. For this example I'm sticking with all companies yielding no more than 2.0 percent and want to end up with eight.

I see Automatic Data Processing, a computer software company, with a 0.9 percent yield. ADP is near the top of the heap, with forty-seven back-to-back years of higher earnings and twenty-two of dividends, the sixth-best record of all companies. Even more amazing, the company has posted 149 straight quarters of double-digit earnings growth. Although I can't prove it, that has to be the best record in the world. I know it's the best in this country.

I don't want more than one company starting with an A (you can have more than one if you like) so I skip to the Bs and find Bandag (auto parts) is the first B company meeting the 2.0 percent yield criterion. Bandag has one of the strongest balance sheets of any company, with equity being more than 70 percent of total assets. Then I go to the Cs. There, Century Telephone yields 1 percent.

In the Ds I find Diebold Inc. with a 1.1 percent yield.

The first company in the Es, Eaton Vance (financial industry), has a 1.4 percent yield and sixteen years in a row of
higher dividends per share. Fastenal Corp. pays no dividend and qualifies for inclusion in the portfolio.

Now I have six companies and need only two more to
get eight. Gannett, a major force in newspapers and one
of Warren Buffett's holdings, is in the Gs and sports a 1.4
percent yield. To round out the list, I spot Hannaford
Brothers, a grocery chain, with a 1.6 percent yield.

Now I buy the portfolio and invest 12.5 percent of my
money in each. One year from the purchase date, I add
additional money to the portfolio and bring the bottom
two or three laggard positions into line with the others. If
one stock, let's say it's Bandag, runs way ahead of the rest
of the pack and becomes dramatically overweighted, I
don't sell part of it to bring it into line with the other seven
because I don't want to pay capital-gains taxes. I let my
profits ride. As long as I don't realize them, my money
continues to grow tax-deferred with the exception of taxes
I'll pay on annual dividends. That won't be a lot because
the yield is a skimpy 1.2 percent.

COMPANY	INDUSTRY	YIELD
Automatic Data Processing	Computer Software	0.9%
Bandag Inc.	Auto Parts	2.0
Century Telephone	Telephone	1.0
Diebold Inc.	Office Equipment	1.1
Eaton Vance	Financial	1.4
Fastenal Corp.	Retail	0.0
Gannett Co.	Publishing	1.4
Hannaford Brothers	Grocery	1.6
	Average	1.2%

If I want to pay no taxes, I need eight companies that don't pay dividends. They're just as easy to find as stocks with meager yields although there aren't nearly as many from which to choose. This is a totally tax-deferred portfolio—just like a retirement plan—so long as I never sell and take a capital gain. One big advantage is I have instant access to my money in case I need it. There's no early-withdrawal penalty as there is with a retirement plan.

In a taxable account, there are only two good reasons ever to sell one of your stocks. The first is if the stock is deleted from America's Finest Companies. In that case you sell the deleted stock and replace it with another in America's Finest Companies. The second reason to sell is that you need the money. Other than these, there isn't a good reason to sell unless one of your stocks has a loss, and you'd like to use the loss to offset other income. In a nontaxable account, the loss wouldn't be recognized.

It's important for you always to picture yourself as a buyer, not a seller, especially in a taxable account. Once your portfolio is set up, you want to keep buying more of what you've got and keep all stock positions in as near equal proportion as possible. Sell only when necessary. Otherwise Uncle Sam (and probably the state where you reside) will come calling to claim his "fair" share of *your* profits. Why pay taxes when you don't have to? Avoid them by letting your portfolio continue to appreciate over the next five, ten, fifteen, twenty years or more.

Multibillionaire Warren Buffett is a buyer of quality, and he rarely sells. Since he's worth more than $18 billion and is one of the world's wealthiest individuals, what he knows is worth knowing. Buffett says, "Buying only the

best is something that . . . is very simple and very obvious."
He also says his favorite holding period is "forever."

If you invest strictly in America's Finest Companies and continue to buy more of what you own and rarely sell, then you are modeling Buffett, the finest example of a successful long-term investor. Maybe you won't be worth $18 billion before you die (then again maybe you will), but you could easily become a millionaire, even a multi-millionaire, with enough time and patience.

To start building a secure financial future with a portfolio of stocks in America's Finest Companies, to continue buying them, and to hold them for a long time is such a simple (I call it a no-brainer) strategy you have to wonder why everyone doesn't do it.

CHAPTER TEN

If You've Never Invested Before, It's Easy to Get Started

If you've invested before, you've already got a brokerage account and know how it works and the commissions and fees involved. But if you're just beginning, the prospect of opening an account can be intimidating, particularly if you've got only a few hundred or a few thousand dollars to invest. You may think you're such a small investor nobody will want to do business with you. It's true a lot of brokers aren't interested in accounts that "small" because they think they don't make enough commissions. What a shortsighted view! These brokers fail to realize that large accounts usually don't start large; they start small. If one broker doesn't seem interested, hang up and try another one. There are plenty who will gladly accept your business, and they're not hard to find.

You can normally open an account with any stockbroker by phone. Jack White is open twenty-four hours a day every day and advertises that it is the "West Coast's first discount broker," with continuous service since 1973. Based on surveys conducted by *Smart Money* and *The Wall Street Journal Magazine of Personal Business*, Jack White was named number one overall in 1994, 1995, and again in 1996 (Waterhouse Securities was number one in 1997) in a survey of the twenty largest discount brokers. In just a few minutes you give the broker enough background information (nothing confidential or revealing) to activate your account and then place your initial order to buy shares of America's Finest Companies. Opening a new account is that simple, and costs nothing but a few minutes' time.

Discount brokers generally offer lower commission rates than full-service brokers because they're seeking investors who want to save money and who, like you, make their own investment decisions. Charles Schwab (800-435-4000) is the largest, but there are others with a national presence, including Quick & Reilly (800-221-5220), Olde Discount (800-USA-OLDE), Pacific Brokerage (800-421-8395), Waterhouse (800-765-5185), and Jack White & Co. (800-431-3500).

The good news about discount brokers is that more and more are cropping up around the country. Your bank may have a discount brokerage operation, as do quite a few of the banks in my hometown. If it does, you can get more information at any of the bank's branches. Many discounters are local, have rock-bottom commission rates, and advertise little if at all. They usually don't find you. You have to find them. A good place to start is the Yellow Pages or on the World Wide Web.

Full-service national firms are led by Merrill Lynch (800-MER-RILL) and Smith Barney (212-698-6000), the two brokers with the largest sales forces. They're trailed by a number of smaller but high-quality regional firms scattered across the country in cities like San Francisco, Dallas, St. Petersburg, Minneapolis, Atlanta, Charlotte, and Richmond. What all these firms have in common is they usually have the highest commissions and fees, but they also offer services the discounters don't offer, like stock and bond research. They also sell an array of financial products, including life insurance and annuities.

Since you're now your own money manager and are comfortable with your own decisions about what and when to buy and sell, where you open a brokerage account isn't nearly as important as it would be if you had no idea what you were doing. You do know what you're doing. You're in control, not the broker. There's no need to worry about a salesman selling you something you don't want because you won't let him.

What is important is that the firm is reputable and has the services you need. Just as important is how much they charge. Most brokers have a fixed minimum commission in the $25 to $50 range regardless of the transaction size. The average is about $40. If you buy one share of each of five stocks, total commissions could be as low as $100, as high as $250, and on average around $200. One of my clients wanted to buy $200 of stock for each of her four grandchildren and have the shares registered in their names. After a lot of shopping, she found the lowest commission rate at the discount-brokerage arm of her bank.

Since the first edition of this book in January 1995 there are now more options available for small investors than ever before. The financial newspapers and magazines are full of ads, and the ads change frequently so that some of what you're reading now may already be out of date. This is by no means a comprehensive list of what's available but it is a good overview of the choices investors have.

Charles Schwab introduced a program called "e.Schwab." in 1996 proclaiming "low commissions of just $39 for stock trades up to 1,000 shares and just three cents a share for additional shares." The firm gives you the software to access your portfolio, create charts and graphs, and get company reports and quotes twenty-four hours a day, every day. You also gain access to Reuters Money Network and S&P MarketScope. For information call 800/ 372-4922 ext. 126.

Smallish Kennedy Cabot of Beverly Hills (800/252-0090) seems to be a firm that will always help the small investor, even if he or she purchases only one share of stock at the time. Established in 1960, the firm runs big ads in many of the national financial media. They say they are the first brokerage firm to offer IRA/Keogh accounts with no minimum deposit requirements and no set-up or maintenance charges. They offer free dividend reinvestment and margin accounts (where you borrow money to buy additional shares). At press time their commission was just $20 for 1–99 shares of any stock at any price and $30 for 100–600 shares of any stock at any price. The cost to register and mail a stock certificate is just $3. Each account is insured for up to $50 million. That should take care of most of us.

Prudential Securities (800/654-5454 ext. 400) has been pushing its no-fee IRA with a yearly contribution of $250 or more. Ceres Securities (800/628-6100) advertises you can trade any common or preferred stock, any number of shares, for one flat rate—$18. But there is a catch—you must have $5,000 or more equity in your account. A free services at the Ceres web site is a daily commentary from business columnist Andrew Tobias.

Waterhouse Securities (800/590-8899) of New York offers a free brochure about the company's commissions and services. They're running a lot of ads touting Touch-Tone trading to save an additional 10% on commissions, free mutual-fund investing, free investment information, free dividend reinvestment, and free IRAs with no fees, no minimums. The firm will either hold your securities in custody or deliver them to you without charge.

Fidelity Investments (800/544-0003) has an Ultra Service Account with no annual fee, discounted commissions for all customers, brokers available every day, and a minimum investment of $10,000. As do many firms, they throw in unlimited checkwriting, a VISA checking card, and one "easy-to-read" statement.

There are numerous other firms that advertise often, including E*Trade (800/786-2573) and National Discount (800/4-1-PRICE), but this may already be more than you ever wanted to know. If it's not, there are other sources you can check out, probably for free at your local library. See the December 25, 1995 *Fortune* article, "Get the Best Deal From Your Broker." You can also check into the American Association of Individual Investors' "Guide to

Discount Brokerage Firms." Another source well worth checking is the annual *Smart Money* review of discount brokers. The July 1997 issue evaluates twenty-one firms in nine different categories ranging from trading costs to breadth of products to on-line trading to staying out of trouble.

There's an outfit called the National Council of Individual Investors that ranks brokers (even those of banks) based on mathematical weightings of data from four areas: breadth of service, commissions/fees, disciplinary record, and stock-performance record. They found that on the whole bank brokerages are cheaper than full-service brokers. No surprise there. They also found that quite a few firms will charge $25 and more for registering and delivering a stock certificate. That adds up to a lot if you buy one share each of five different companies, pay a commission to buy each, and then on top of that pay $25 per certificate to have it mailed to you. NCII's number is 800/663-8516.

When you begin an investment program with as little as $500, commissions, transaction fees, and other charges can be a real burden because they can take a good chunk out of principal. But as you continue to add to your portfolio every six months to a year and your assets multiply, they become less and less of an albatross. Although it's important to reduce or eliminate every cost possible, it's of far greater importance to have your portfolio invested strictly in America's Finest Companies, keep the holdings properly weighted, and buy more of what you already own every chance you get.

In my twenty-six years in the investment business, I've seen people fail to make a lot of money because they spent so much time shopping for the best broker, or trying to

unearth the best brokerage firm, or attempting to cut commissions to the bone, or all three. They were putting the
cart before the horse, and that's not a profitable strategy.
Investing for maximum profits requires patience, a simple
strategy like the one unfurled in these pages, and at least
a ten-year horizon to give the strategy ample time to work.
Keeping costs minimal improves your overall return,
there's no doubt about that, but it won't improve your return nearly so much as planning to beat Wall Street with
America's Finest Companies, implementing your plan,
and sticking to your plan.

CHAPTER ELEVEN

How to Turn Your Children or Grandchildren into Savvy Investors and Make Them Millionaires in the Process

The day after my daughter was born in 1978, I opened a custodial account for her at the brokerage firm where I was director of equity research. A custodial account is as simple to open as a regular brokerage account. An adult signs on as "custodian" until the child is eighteen, at which time the account is under the complete control of the child, who, of course, by then is a young adult. Anyone can contribute up to $10,000 of cash, securities, or a combination of the two to a custodial account every year with no gift-tax consequences.

Once the account was set up, my wife and I contributed a few thousand dollars, and then I made three very important phone calls, to my father, my mother, and my aunt, who's like a second mother. Since this was their first grandchild by me, I told them I was certain they'd each want to help secure Gracie's financial future with gifts of cash or stock. Naturally they couldn't say no. It wasn't long before those gifts came in the mail, and I was able to add several thousand dollars of stock to Gracie's account. Before she was even six months old, she had a five-digit sum in her brokerage account, which I invested in a portfolio of growth stocks. There was no America's Finest Companies back then, but I could still pick stocks to beat the market. I knew Gracie was off on a sound financial footing.

Since then my father and aunt made some additional gifts of stock, but the account is worth what it is today (about $175,000) primarily because her portfolio has performed so well. I don't know how much money has been withdrawn to pay for private-school education, but she started in kindergarten and is now in college. Average tuition taken out per year must have been at least $9,000, so you can see the portfolio has been a real winner.

When my son, Will, was born in 1989, I immediately opened a custodial account for him as I did for his sister. Although he didn't get off to a five-digit start as she had done, he's still in excellent financial shape and already has a greater net worth than most Americans.

Once Will is eighteen, the money in his account is his to do with as he pleases. That's the law as long as he's legally competent, and I have no reason to think he won't be. I hope he'll let me help him manage his money until he gets through college, as I'm helping his sister, but he doesn't have to. Even though his account is for his education, he doesn't have to spend the assets for that purpose.

He can dispose of them any way he wishes once he is of age.

I want both my children to have secure financial futures. There should be more than enough money left over in their accounts after four years of college (perhaps graduate school, too) to be able to achieve that goal. Gracie will graduate from college in the spring of 2000. (I went on record in my newsletter in fall 1990 saying the Dow will be at 10000 by then. Let's hope I'm right.)

Assuming college expenses at a liberal $20,000 per year and 13 percent growth (before taxes) in the portfolio, she ought to have about $250,000 to work with when she graduates. If that money grows at a modest 9 percent a year after taxes and she doesn't tap into it, it will be worth close to $2.8 million when she's 50 and well over $6.5 million when she's 60. At 10 percent after tax, which is certainly achievable, the numbers will be $3.6 million at age 50 and nearly $9.5 million by age 60.

I'll encourage Gracie to open an IRA and put every dime she earns into it (up to $2,000 annually) while she's in college. When I was in school, I was fortunate to have my father pay all tuition and other expenses. The $3,000 or so I earned working for the student newspaper was mine to save or spend. Had I known anything about investing, I probably would have set at least part of it aside. Instead I spent it. That's okay. I had a lot of fun. If Gracie earns $100 per month nine months per year during her four years in college, and she invests it in an IRA compounding at 13 percent annually, that little $3,600 investment will swell to nearly $500,000 by the time she's 60. Even better, if she contributes the maximum $2,000 annu-

182

ally from age 22 through age 60, her IRA will multiply to $2.3 million.

An IRA is a powerful wealthbuilder for anyone, especially a child. The younger the child the more valuable the IRA is. Suppose Will begins to do odd jobs like mowing lawns (as I did) when he's 10 and mows five each week during the summer (again as I did). I made $7 a week back in the 1950s. Will can probably make at least ten times that. Let's say he rakes in $75 weekly for ten weeks each summer, starting at age 10 and ending when he turns 16. At 16 he'll drive a car and be much "too old" to mow lawns. For each of the six years he works, Will will put the entire $750 into his IRA, which will earn 13 percent annually through age 65. That's only $4,500, but it will surge to $2.8 million over 49 years. Will will become a millionaire from mowing lawns for just six years. Since this money will be in an IRA, the principal will grow without being taxed until Will begins to withdraw it.

I assume Will will be like a lot of young people and want to spend most of his income. Or worse, he'll be like I was. I spent everything I earned and then asked (begged?) my parents and grandparents for more. The words *saving* and *investing* meant nothing to me. I want them to mean something for my children.

To offset Will's urge to spend what he earns while in high school, I'll offer to match it. It will be either a dollar-for-dollar match or a two-for-one match, probably the latter. Under a two-for-one match, for every dollar Will invests in his IRA I'll give him a dollar to spend as he wishes. I'll also invest a dollar in his custodial account. While he's putting $4,500 from mowing lawns into his IRA, I'll be pumping $4,500 into his custodial account. Using a conservative aftertax return of 9 percent, the $4,500 from me will be worth $306,981 when he is 65. But if I invest all the money in non-dividend-paying stocks and sell rarely and the money grows at 13 percent like the IRA, it will grow to about $1.8 million. With my small gifts and Will's small contribution to his IRA, he'll amass close to $4.6 million by age 65.

If I were to sit in a room with parents and grandparents and we discussed whether they should provide for their children's financial security, assuming they are able to, there'd probably be a heated argument within a few minutes. Some would say providing financial security works to a child's detriment because the child doesn't learn how to fend for himself in the real world. My friend Eddie Graham feels exactly like that. He grew up poor and worked hard all his life to make ends meet. His house is paid for, he still manages to set aside a little extra money each month, and he and his wife like to junket to Las Vegas and Atlantic City regularly to enjoy, in his words, "the good life." When I asked Eddie about his children, he said he planned to leave nothing to them. It was up to them to "work hard and provide for themselves" just as he's done. That's one view.

Another is that parents and grandparents should offer some financial aid but should not try, even if they can afford it, to provide everything monetary a child needs. And still a third view is my view. I want to make my children as financially comfortable as I can before they enter the workplace, which I assume both will do eventually. Why? Because I'd like both of them to have the opportunity to enjoy the kinds of careers they can sink their teeth into and not have to worry about whether the job pays enough.

I want Will to become a high school history teacher if that's what he really wants, even though teachers, in my opinion, are grossly underpaid for what they render to society. If Gracie wants to be an artist, I don't want her to "starve" while she pursues her dream.

Using my children as examples, I'm demonstrating the relative ease with which all children can build small fortunes, even large ones. They can do so without your help if they have the knowledge within these pages, but it will be considerably easier with your assistance. A custodial account at a brokerage is a great starting place. If you're worried that your children or grandchildren will be foolish with their money after they reach 18, you can, for modest fees, establish trust accounts that are very flexible yet have restrictions preventing the assets from being abused. You can be the trustee and invest the money however you like. In either a custodial or a trust account, you'll want to invest strictly in America's Finest Companies. If your child or grandchild is eight or older, he or she will most likely want to participate in assembling the portfolio. Sometimes children even younger than that willingly cooperate. All you need to do is ask them.

Remember the example of my daughter, who invested in eight companies she chose herself in 1988. Through July 31, 1997, they've beat the S & P by 53 percent. Gracie was excited about having the chance to pick companies. She wasn't interested in why she was doing it. She just knew it was fun. Money is fun to most children and young people (as it should be with us adults), so why not take advantage of that?

As I said in a previous chapter, I teach applied economics to juniors and seniors where my daughter went to school. I'm the real-life "consultant" who takes practical experiences and knowledge into the classroom to bring economics to life for these bright young adults. Junior Achievement writes its own economics text, which is revised and updated every three years. If you've ever hankered to learn more about the "dismal science" but couldn't find an interesting, readable text, JA's is it, the most useful economics text I've ever studied.

With every group of students, I spend two to three sessions on investing, using the principles outlined here. One exercise I emphasize is having them pick five companies they'd like to invest in. There are only three rules. One, the companies must be high quality. Two, they must have dividend reinvestment plans. The students don't know whether the companies have DRPs or not, so they keep picking until they come up with five that do. Three, they have to hold these companies for twenty years. They cannot sell (unless there's a buyout and they're forced to) during the period, but they can buy more of the stocks whenever they get additional money.

Each of the classes I've worked with to date has picked a good portfolio. McDonald's, PepsiCo or Coca-Cola, Wal-Mart, and Merck or Bristol-Myers Squibb have been popular choices.

A five-stock portfolio is easily put together at very little cost. Let's say the child wants to buy Walgreen, Coca-Cola, Colgate-Palmolive, Kellogg, and William Wrigley Jr. All have DRPs and you need buy only one share of each to begin participating. One broker you can call to execute your orders is Kennedy Cabot (800)252-0090. The firm is good with small transactions. If you buy one share of each of these five, you'll spend about $365, plus total commissions around $125, based on prices at this date. Get the shares registered in the child's name, with you or another adult as custodian, and have them delivered to your home. Each company will mail a simple form so you can check the block required to participate in the company's dividend reinvestment plan. Additional share purchases can be made through the companies' optional investment plans (OCPs), which generally carry no commission, or a small one at worst.

To make the investing process even more fun for the child, you should know that some companies offer freebies to shareholders. Every December, Wrigley sends all shareholders a box of twenty-five-stick packs of gum hand-picked by Mr. Wrigley himself. Hershey Foods has a toll-free number shareholders can use to order gifts for friends and relatives. Anheuser-Busch has a Theme Parks Club for shareholders allowing 10–15 percent discounts at the country's facilities scattered across the country. To be eligible for these perks, the shares must be registered in the name of the shareholder and cannot be held by a broker.

Colgate-Palmolive's new shareowners get a packet of discount coupons, which may or may not be fun for a child to receive. This will depend on the age of the child and what the coupons are for, but I guarantee the parent or grandparent will find them useful. Ditto for H. J. Heinz. CSX owns the world-famous Greenbrier resort. Shareholders can stay there at discounted rates. Minnesota Mining & Manufacturing sends its new shareholders a variety of Post-It notes, tape, and other accessories, while Kimberly-Clark provides the chance to buy a bag of its products at well off the regular retail price.

I'd never suggest buying one of these companies just

for its perks, but the perks do make ownership more fun, especially for children. Children have to have fun while they're learning to invest. Otherwise they won't be interested. And come to think of it, having fun while you invest isn't a bad idea for adults either. Beating Wall Street with America's Finest Companies is the most fun way I know.

CHAPTER TWELVE

How to Use America's Finest Companies Statistics for Maximum Profits

This book shows you a simple, time-proven way to make your money grow at an above-average rate with practically no risk. By investing solely in America's Finest Companies, you can safely double your money every five to six years and beat 75 percent of all investment professionals 100 percent of the time.

As I pointed out in chapter 1, a diversified portfolio in America's Finest Companies should give you a 13–15 percent compound annual return compared to 12 percent, the market's rate for the past fifty years. That 1–3 percent advantage over a long period of time is worth hundreds of thousands of extra dollars.

BILL STATON

If you invest $50 per month at 12 percent for your child at birth and continue through age 18, his money will grow to $38,272 as the 19th birthday approaches. With no additional contributions from you or the child, that $38,272 will be worth $1,438,328 when he or she is 50; $4,467,228 at age 60; and $13,874,532 by age 70. These are staggering numbers, aren't they? You're probably asking yourself, "But isn't $13,874,532 at age 70 more than enough for anyone?" My answer is "It would sure be more than enough for me, by many millions."

My mission is to try to have you earn as much money as you can on your investments, as safely as you can, and in as little time as you can. I'd rather see you earn 13 percent per year than 12 percent. Fourteen percent would be even better and 15 percent even better than that. I believe 13–15 percent is reasonable. Beyond that, we go into the never-never land of returns that may never materialize, but are frequently promoted by others in the financial arena.

Why not earn as much money as possible? The more you earn, the more you'll have to spend on things you need, things you want, and for helping others, too. I'm not unreasonable or impractical. I know most of us don't save and invest every extra dollar and never spend it. We save and invest, or at least try to, in a manner that lets us spend part of our principal each year while leaving the balance to grow for the future.

Let's go back to the previous example, in which no money is withdrawn until at least age 50, and develop another example that mimics real life. In this instance, the young person is worth $38,272 when he's 18 and needs some money from his account for college, $8,000 per year for four years. The parents make up the difference. After taking out $8,000 for first-year expenses, $30,272 is left to grow at 12 percent, the market's historic return, until the next year, when another $8,000 is withdrawn, and so forth until the four years are complete. At graduation, the young adult is now 22 and his stockpile has shrunk to $17,399. This amount builds at 12 percent compounded annually. If nothing else is taken out, it will be worth $415,555 when he's 50; $1,290,651 when he's 60; and $4,008,569 when he's 70. But in reality, more will probably be extracted at some point. Maybe it's when he reaches 45 and buys the house of his dreams.

From age 22 to age 45, $17,399 at 12 percent will increase to $235,797. With $150,000 used to purchase the dream house (there'd be a mortgage for the balance), there's $85,797 to grow at a 12 percent annual rate. Five years later at age 50, it has grown to $151,204; to $469,616 at 60; and $1,458,554 at age 70. As a practical matter, money will likely be taken out at various other points from ages 45 to 70, so the end amount may or may not be close to $1,458,554.

If I repeat this illustration, using 13 percent and 15 percent returns, at the end of four years of college the remainder amounts are $18,559 and $20,999, respectively, compared with $17,399. At age 45, after $150,000 is used for the home, $158,574 and $372,696 are left over compared with $85,797. You can see what a huge difference these higher rates are making, even using 13 percent, a figure that's only one percent above the market's 12 percent.

In chapter 8, I said I invested roughly $5,000 (plus commissions) per stock in five different stocks on February

7, 1992, for my son, Will, who was then nearly three. All dividends have been reinvested since inception. To date, Will's portfolio has knocked down a better return than the market. What I'm saying works in theory and, most important, in practice, too. I successfully invest for myself and my children and outpace the market virtually every year, using the companies in America's Finest Companies. You can do it, too.

Someone once said, "The easiest way to end up with a small fortune is to start with a large one." I've proved the opposite to be true. You can end up with a large fortune by beginning with as little as $50 each month and earning the market's rate of return. By outstripping the market, the fortune will be even larger.

Of course these "case-study returns" assume no taxes, but that's not uncommon. Taxes are excluded whenever returns are discussed, whether they be for the market, a mutual fund, or a portfolio manager. We all know taxes are impossible to avoid. They can be heavily reduced but never completely eliminated.

They also assume the investment program begins at birth. That's fine if you've got a baby or grandbaby, but it won't do you any personal good because you're almost certainly years, if not decades, behind. It's still not too late even if you're 50 and have done little or nothing for your future. Will an extra 1 to 3 percent per year really make a difference to your financial security? You bet!

To illustrate, you're already covered by a retirement plan at work but have extra money and decide to invest $2,000 each year in your IRA. If you equal the market and earn 12 percent annually, you'll have $39,309 after 10 years; $83,506 after 15; and $161,397 after 20. If you earn

13 percent, the numbers will be $41,628 in 10 years; $91,343 in 15; and $182,940 in 20. Using a 15 percent return, you'll have $46,699 at the end of 10 years; $109,435 in 15; and $235,620 at the end of 20 years.

Over a twenty-year period, the difference between a 12 percent and a 15 percent return is $74,223, 46 percent more. I'd say that's sizable, wouldn't you? The difference is even more dramatic if you have a SEP or Keogh and can kick in a lot more than $2,000 per year. What if the amount is $10,000 annually instead of $2,000 and you begin at age 50? At 12 percent per year, you'll build an $806,987 nest egg. At 13 percent, the nest egg will be $914,699. At 15 percent, it will be $1,178,101—$371,114 more than if you earned 12 percent.

Any way I've measured it, a diversified portfolio invested in America's Finest Companies has substantially outperformed the market over the past ten years. This means they've whomped most of the pros, too, since the market indexes beat three-quarters of them year in and year out. It's easy to see why they're market beaters. Each of the 397 companies qualifying for listing has increased dividends and/or earnings for at least ten straight years.

It's easy to explain how America's Finest Companies are above-average performers. They're growing, and the value of their businesses is on a consistent uptrend. As the values of the businesses rise, the stock prices rise also. They have to. Here's why.

Look at this staircase. It begins on the left of the page and rises one step at a time until it gets to the right side, all the while getting taller and taller. This staircase could represent any of America's Finest Companies. Every step

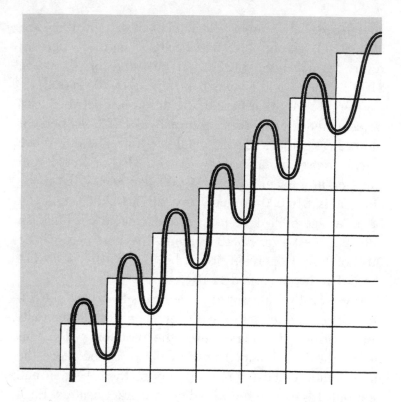

represents another increase in the value of the AFC company's business.

Now look at the curve. This represents an AFC stock price over the years. It goes up and down in value (randomly) in the short run, but the path is always in only one direction—upward. Sometimes the stock price is above what the company is really worth. At other times it's valued about correctly. And at still other times it's undervalued.

If you're dollar-cost averaging, as I strongly urge—purchasing the stock of an AFC company over five, ten, fifteen years, and more—you'll buy at different points along the stair steps. Maybe sometimes you'll pay too much. When you do, you'll buy fewer shares per dollar invested because the price is high. Often you'll buy shares on the cheap and for the same dollars invested will be able to load up. Given enough time, dollar-cost averaging will automatically produce superior results in contrast to a buy-and-hold strategy, as demonstrated in chapter 7.

There are many ways to use the data here so that you end up with a well-balanced portfolio to meet your needs. You'll be a winner regardless of how you select your portfolio. Selecting can be as simple and easy as throwing darts. You could make copies of each of the statistical pages and post them on a wall you don't mind having a few holes in (in case you miss a throw or two). Next toss some darts, however many you require, one dart per company. Then buy the companies the darts strike.

One excellent portfolio you can buy outright or pick from is the fifteen Dow stocks (there are thirty that make up the venerable Dow Jones industrial average) that made the AFC cutoff. These are some of the oldest, strongest, most respected names in American industry. They've been around a long time, and you can rest assured they'll be around a lot longer. All have roots stretching back decades before the Great Depression, with the exception of McDonald's, the rookie of the group.

This is not only a well-diversified group of companies, it's a high-caliber group as well. Eight of the fifteen are ranked A+ (highest) by Standard & Poor's, which establishes its rankings in a computerized system based on earnings and dividend records over the past decade. Sta-

COMPANY	YEARS OF HIGHER EARNINGS	YEARS OF HIGHER DIVIDENDS	S & P RANKING	DIVDS. PAID SINCE
Coca-Cola	22	39	A+	1893
Disney, Walt Co.	0	11	A	1957
DuPont	3	14	B+	1904
Exxon	2	14	A−	1882
General Electric	21	21	A+	1899
McDonald's	32	22	A+	1976
Merck and Company	3	21	A+	1935
Minnesota Mining & Manufacturing	5	38	A+	1916
J. P. Morgan	2	20	B+	1892
Philip Morris	3	31	A+	1928
Procter & Gamble	3	41	A	1891
Hewlett-Packard	5	10	A	1965
Johnson & Johnson	38	34	A+	1905
Travelers Group	2	10	A	1986
Wal-Mart Stores	35	13	A+	1973

bility is a key variable. Four are rated A, one A— (above average) and two B+ (average).

It's easy to get together a portfolio using any one, or an assortment of, variables. Do you want stocks that yield at least 4 percent? Do you like stocks selling for $25 or less? Or maybe you'd feel better owning only the companies ranked A+ by Standard & Poor's. You can choose them from the list in the appendix. Other selection criteria are industry, the price/earnings ratio, and the number of consecutive years of higher earnings and dividends.

You might like to make up your own combination of several variables, i.e., stocks priced between $20 and $40 per share, with P/E ratios no greater than 20, yields of at least 3 percent, and at least fifteen years of higher dividends. It's up to you. The important thing to keep in mind is that however you build your portfolio, you're building it with the *crème de la crème* of corporations, the elite, America's Finest.

Now I'll tell you how to get more out of the data in the appendix. All the companies are listed alphabetically along with their stock symbols (column 1). An (A) follows a company's symbol if it trades on the American Stock Exchange.

After the stock symbol is the industry category in column 2. Regardless of the size of your stock portfolio—five, eight, ten, twelve, or more companies—each should be in a different industry. If you want to pick an eight-stock portfolio, there's no faster way than turning to any page of the company's listings in the appendix and going down it company by company until you have the right number in diverse industries.

Column 3 shows the price of the stock when this book

(1) COMPANY/STOCK SYMBOL	(2) INDUSTRY	(3) PRICE	(4) PRICE/EARNINGS RATIO	(5) YIELD (%)	(6) DIVD. REINVEST. PLAN
Abbott Laboratories/ABT	Health Care	44	19.3	2.2	X

(7) CONSECUTIVE ANNUAL EARNINGS INCREASES	(8) CONSECUTIVE ANNUAL DIVIDEND INCREASES	(9) S & P RANKING	(10) ADDRESS/PHONE NUMBER
24	23	A+	100 Abbott Park Rd., Abbott Park, IL 60064 847-937-6100

went to press. Column 4 gives the P/E ratio, which is the stock price divided by the latest twelve months' earnings. It's well documented that over longer periods of time a portfolio of stocks (culled from a large-enough group) with below-average price/earnings ratios consistently beats that group. For example, the eight lowest P/Es in the Dow Jones average regularly beat the Dow average of thirty stocks over one-, five-, and ten-year periods.

The first evidence I saw that this is true was in a paper written by Benjamin Graham, my financial hero. He cited research by the old brokerage firm of Drexel & Company in Philadelphia. Their 1965 study concluded that in twenty-two of the twenty-eight years since 1936 the ten lowest-P/E Dow stocks outdistanced the Dow.

If you'd like to track America's Finest Companies yearly, including the lowest-P/E stocks, I invite you to become a member of The Staton Institute^{SM} Inc. and receive my monthly newsletter, plus a host of other benefits. There's a membership application on page 255.

Column 5 shows the dividend yield for each stock if the company pays a dividend. Investing in stocks with above-average dividend yields is a conservative—but sound— way to make your money grow while simultaneously reducing downside risk and volatility. When you invest in the highest-quality companies like those shown in the back of the book and reinvest all your dividends, your returns will usually be equal to, or better than, the Dow Jones and S & P 500 indexes.

Column 6 shows whether a company has a dividend reinvestment plan. If the company reinvests dividends and optional cash payments at a discount to market price, the discount is shown in parentheses beside the X.

Columns 7 and 8 show the number of years of back-to-back earnings and dividend increases. I haven't found any correlation between the length of a company's string of earnings and/or dividends and its stock price performance, but some people are more comfortable investing in companies with the longer records, like American Home Products, Emerson Electric, Johnson & Johnson, RPM, and Tootsie Roll Industries.

Column 9 provides the S & P rankings. The most consistent companies are ranked B + and higher although Standard & Poor's has no ranking for some.

To contact a company for more information or to inquire about its DRP, use the address, phone number, or web site in column 10. If a toll-free number is available, it's included.

CHAPTER THIRTEEN

Chance Favors Only the Mind That Is Prepared

When my daughter was five, her favorite book was *The Value of Believing in Yourself: The Story of Louis Pasteur* by Spencer Johnson, M.D. (Few people know Johnson coauthored *The One-Minute Manager.*) It's one of my favorite books, too. I know his story almost by heart, having read it aloud several dozen times.

Pasteur (1822–95), as you may recall from your history courses, was a chemist and bacteriologist whose scientific exploits were widely ignored, since he was not a medical doctor. Pasteur had the firm conviction that diseases were caused by invisible enemies called germs or bacteria. Even though many of the finest minds in the world had no faith in his work, Pasteur believed in himself. He uncovered a cure for silkworm disease and later for anthrax and rabies. He also invented pasteurization, the process of heating milk to 140 degrees Fahrenheit for thirty minutes, then quickly cooling it.

Throughout the book, Louis Pasteur repeats to himself, "I believe I can, I believe I can," as he vigorously hunts for the rabies cure. He had to believe in himself because few others beside his wife, Marie, did. But Pasteur knew exactly what he was doing. Some of his critics refused to acknowledge his great works because they thought Louis Pasteur was just lucky. Pasteur knew luck had nothing to do with his outstanding accomplishments and said, "Chance favors only the mind that is prepared."

The average man or woman on the street thinks investing in stocks is nothing but a game of chance. The luckiest ones make money. The rest lose it. They don't realize that investing in stocks is the fastest way to accumulate wealth and that it can be done with virtually zero risk, as I've demonstrated.

If you'll use the simple, rational method I've outlined, you'll have phenomenal success with your money regardless of the amount you begin with. In a sense, you'll be like Louis Pasteur because you'll ignore the advice commonly given by most financial experts, who want you to believe you need them to be successful. There aren't many of us who know you can do it yourself, have a lot of fun, and make a lot of money, too. Believe in yourself. You can do it!

In building a diversified portfolio of America's Finest Companies, you're doing far more than buying pieces of paper that change in price many times each day. You are actually buying pieces of American enterprises, the best this country has to offer. As these companies grow and thrive in the future, so will you by virtue of your ownership.

Does it really matter if the value of your shares goes down today and then bobs up tomorrow? Of course not. Value is not created in a day. Value takes years to build. Daily fluctuations in stock prices are meaningless. They do not affect the long-term value of the Finest Companies.

What does affect the value is growth in revenue, earnings, dividends, and the asset values of the businesses. If you continually add to your portfolio of first-rate companies, you can be certain that over the years the value will increase faster than from other investments—and keep you well ahead of inflation and the tax man, too.

There's nothing to wait for. You now have the knowledge you need for investing and stock-market success. Epicurus warned, "Life is wasted in procrastination."

Procrastinate no longer. Start the steps to financial security today.

Happy investing!

Appendix: List of the 397 America's Finest Companies

Company Name/Stock Symbol	Industry	Price	P/E	YIELD	Dividend Reinvestment Plan	Year High EPS	Year High Dividend	S&P Rank	Address/Phone Number
Abbott Laboratories/ABT	Health Care	63	24.5	1.5%	X	25	24	A+	100 Abbott Park Rd., Abbott Park IL 60064 847/937-6100 www.abbott.com
ABM Industries Inc./ABM	Special Services	22	20.6	1.8%		9	32	A	50 Fremont St., San Francisco CA 94105 415/597-4500 www.abm.com
AFLAC Inc./AFL	Insurance/Life	53	18.7	0.9%	X	7	14	A	1932 Wynnton Rd., Columbus GA 31999 800/227-4756 www.aflac.com
Air Products & Chemicals/APD	Chemicals	85	23.5	1.4%	X	3	14	A	7201 Hamilton Blvd., Allentown PA 18195 610/481-5775 www.airproducts.com
Alberto-Culver Co./ACV	Personal Care	27	23.3	0.7%		5	12	A	2525 Armitage Ave., Melrose Park IL 60160 708/450-3005
Albertson's Inc./ABS	Grocery	38	19.5	1.7%	X	27	25	A+	PO Box 20, Boise ID 83726 208/395-6200
Allegheny Power System Inc./AYP	Electric Utility	29	14.9	5.9%	X	0	38	A−	10435 Downsville Pike, Hagerstown MD 21740 301/665-2713 www.alleghenypower.com

Company	Industry								Address
ALLIED Group Inc./GRP	Insurance/Prop.	43	17.8	1.6%	X	0	10	A	701 Fifth Ave., Des Moines IA 50391 800/532-1436 www.alliedgroupinc.com
ALLTEL Corp./AT	Telephone	32	19.8	3.2%	X	o	36	A	One Allied Dr., Little Rock AR 77202 501/661-8999 www.alltel.com
American Business Products/ABP	Ofc. Equip./Supp.	24	17.1	2.6%	X	0	39	A	PO Box 105684, Atlanta GA 30348 800/227-3390
American General Corp./AGC	Financial	50	17.7	2.8%	X	3	21	B+	PO Box 3247, Houston TX 77253 800/242-1111 www.agc.com
American Heritage Life/AHL	Insurance/Life	36	17.9	2.2%	X	22	27	A	1776 Amer. Heritage Life Dr., Jacksonville FL 32224 800/874-2532
American Home Products/AHP	Health Care	81	25.6	2.0%	X	44	45	A+	Five Giralda Farms, Madison NJ 07940 201/660-6936
American International Group/AIG	Insurance/Multi.	151	23.6	0.3%		12	11	A+	70 Pine St., New York NY 10270 212/770-6293 www.aig.com
American Natl. Insurance/ANAT	Insurance/Life	91	10.3	2.9%		6	23	A+	One Moody Plaza, Galveston TX 77550 713/763-4661 www.anico.com
American Precision Inds./APR	Electrical Equip.	21	20.8	0.0%		3	19	B+	2777 Walden Ave., Buffalo NY 14225 716/684-9700
American Water Works Co./AWK	Water Utility	22	17.2	3.5%	X	4	21	A	PO Box 1770, Voorhees NJ 08043 609/346-8200
Ameritech Corp./AIT	Telephone	68	17.2	3.3%	X	2	12	A−	30 S. Wacker Dr., Chicago IL 60606 800/257-0902 www.ameritech.com

Company Name/Stock Symbol	Industry	Price	P/E	YIELD	Dividend Reinvestment Plan	Year High EPS	Year High Dividend	S&P Rank	Address/Phone Number
AMP Inc./AMP	Electrical Equip.	47	39.2	2.2%	X	0	43	B+	PO Box 3608, Harrisburg PA 17105 717/592-4267 www.amp.com
AmSouth Bancorporation/ASO	Banking	41	17.4	2.7%	X	2	24	A−	PO Box 11007, Birmingham AL 35288 205/326-5807 www.amsouth.com
Angelica Corp./AGL	Textiles/Apparel	18	23.4	5.3%	X	1	24	B	424 S. Woods Mill Rd., Chesterfield MO 63017 314/854-3800 www.angelica-corp.com
Anheuser-Busch Cos. Inc./BUD	Alcoholic Bever.	48	20.7	2.2%	X	1	22	A	One Busch Place, St. Louis MO 63118 800/342-5283 www.budweiser.com
Aon Corp./AOC	Insurance/Broker	54	50.5	1.9%	X	0	45	A−	123 N. Wacker Dr., Chicago IL 60606 312/701-3000 www.aon.com
Apogee Enterprises Inc./APOG	Bldng. Materials	21	21.2	0.9%		3	22	B	7900 Xerxes Ave. So., Minneapolis MN 55431 612/835-1874
Archer Daniels Midland Co./ADM	Foods	23	18.1	0.9%		0	22	A	PO Box 1470, Decatur IL 62525 217/424-5200 www.admworld.com

Company/Ticker	Industry								Address
Associated Banc-Corp/ ASBC	Banking	39	-4.4	3.0%	X	5	26	A+	PO Box 13307, Green Bay WI 54307 800/236-2722 www.asbc.com
Automatic Data Processing/AUD	Computer Soft.	49	29.3	0.9%		47	22	A+	One ADP Blvd., Roseland NJ 07058 201/994-5000 www.adp.com
Avery Dennison Corp./ AVY	Manufacturing	41	22.2	1.7%	X	6	20	A-	PO Box 7090, Pasadena CA 91109 818/304-2000 www.averydennison.com
Baldor Electric Co./BEZ	Electrical Equip.	30	21.9	1.6%		5	13	A	PO Box 2400, Fort Smith AR 72902 501/646-4711
Banc One Corp./ONE	Banking	50	18.7	3.0%	X	2	24	A+	100 E Broad St., Columbus OH 43271 614/248-6889 www.bankone.com
BancorpSouth Inc./BXS	Banking	30	14.2	2.5%	X	9	14	A	PO Box 789, Tupelo MS 38802 601/680-2000 www.bancorpsouth.com
Bandag Inc./BDG	Auto Parts	51	15.4	2.0%	X	0	20	A	2905 N. Hwy. 61, Muscatine IA 52761 319/262-1400
Bank of Granite Corp./ GRAN	Banking	29	19.6	1.2%	X	43	43	-	PO Box 128, Granite Falls NC 28630 704/496-2022
Banta Corp./BNTA	Printing	29	17.3	1.7%	X	0	19	A-	Box E003, Menasha WI 54952 414/751-7777 www.banta.com
Bard, C.R. Inc./BCR	Medical Prods.	37	23.4	1.9%	X	3	25	A-	730 Central Ave., Murray Hill NJ 07974 908/277-8000
Bausch & Lomb Inc./ BOL	Medical Prods.	43	44.8	2.4%	X	0	10	B+	Rochester NY 14604 800/344-8815 www.bausch.com

Company Name/Stock Symbol	Industry	Price	P/E	YIELD	Dividend Reinvestment Plan	Year High EPS	Year High Dividend	S&P Rank	Address/Phone Number
Bay States Gas Co./BGC	Natural Gas	26	11.1	6.1%	X	1	10	A–	300 Friberg Pkwy., Westborough MA 01581 508/836-7396 www.bgc.com
Baxter International Inc./BAX	Medical Prods.	58	67.4	2.1%	X	1	40	B+	One Baxter Pkwy., Deerfield IL 60015 847/948-4550 www.baxter.com
BB&T Corp./BBK	Banking	50	18.3	2.5%	X(3)	1	24	A–	PO Box 1250, Winston-Salem NC 27102 919/246-4219 www.bbandt.com
Becton, Dickinson & Co./BDX	Medical Prods.	54	23.8	1.0%	X	14	25	A+	1 Becton Dr., Franklin Lakes NJ 07417 800/284-6845
Bell Atlantic Corp./BEL	Telephone	74	18.2	4.0%	X	0	12	A–	1717 Arch St., Philadelphia PA 19103 215/963-6333 www.bell-atl.com
Bemis Co./BMS	Containers	45	22.6	1.8%	X	3	13	A	222 S. Ninth St., Minneapolis MN 55402 612/376-3000
Berkley, W.R. Corp./BKLY	Insurance/Prop.	58	13.0	1.0%		2	15	B+	PO Box 2518, Greenwich CT 06836 203/629-3000 www.wrbc.com
BetzDearborn Inc./BTL	Chemicals	62	32.0	2.4%		0	31	B+	4636 Somerton Rd., Trevose PA 19053 215/953-5550

Company/Ticker	Industry								Address
Biomet Inc./BMET	Medical Prods.	20	21.3	0.0%		18	0	B+	PO Box 587, Warsaw IN 46581 219/267-6639
Black Hills Corp./BKH	Electric Utility	29	13.6	4.9%	X	3	25	A	PO Box 1400, Rapid City SD 57709 605/348-1700
Block, H & R Inc./HRB	Special Services	36	80.0	2.2%	X	0	34	A	4410 Main St., Kansas City MO 64111 816/753-6900 www.hrblock.com
Block Drug Co. Inc./BLOCA	Medical Prods.	46	NMF	2.7%		0	25	A–	257 Cornelison Ave., Jersey City NJ 07302 201/434-3000
Bob Evans Farms Inc./BOBE	Restaurant	17	19.8	1.9%	X	1	33	A–	PO Box 07863, Columbus OH 43207 614/497-4390
Bowl America Inc./BWLA(A)	Entertainment	7	14.9	5.7%		0	24	B+	PO Box 1288, Springfield VA 22151 703/941-6300
Brady, W.H. Co./BRCOA	Chemicals	29	20.9	1.8%	X	4	10	A–	PO Box 751, Milwaukee WI 53201 414/358-6600 www.whbrady.com
Bristol-Myers Squibb Co./BMY	Health Care	82	27.2	1.9%	X	1	24	A	345 Park Ave., New York NY 10154 212/546-4000 www.bms.com
Brooklyn Union Gas Co./BU	Natural Gas	29	19.1	5.0%	X	4	20	A–	1 MetroTech Ctr., Brooklyn NY 11201 718/403-3382 www.bug.com
Brown-Forman Corp./BFB	Alcoholic Bever.	50	20.4	2.2%	X	7	12	A	PO Box 1080, Louisville KY 40201 502/585-1100 www.brown-forman.com
California Water Service Co./CWT	Water Utility	43	11.4	4.9%	X	1	29	A–	1720 N. First St., San Jose CA 95112 408/451-8200

Company Name/Stock Symbol	Industry	Price	P/E	YIELD	Dividend Reinvestment Plan	Year High EPS	Year High Dividend	S&P Rank	Address/Phone Number
Campbell Soup Co./CPB	Foods	51	29.3	1.5%	X	6	22	B+	Campbell Place, Camden NJ 08103 800/909-7687 www.campbellsoups.com
Carlisle Companies Inc./CSL	Manufacturing	39	19.2	1.3%	X	5	20	B+	250 S. Clinton St. #201, Syracuse NY 13202 315/474-2500
CCB Financial Corp./CCB	Banking	80	16.3	2.3%	X	6	32	A	PO Box 931, Durham NC 27702 919/683-7777
Central & South West Corp./CSR	Electric Utility	20	10.5	8.7%	X	0	46	A−	PO Box 660164, Dallas TX 75266 800/527-5797 www.csw.com
Central Louisiana Electric/CNL	Electric Utility	28	13.6	5.6%	X	3	25	A−	PO Box 5000, Pineville LA 71361 800/253-2652 www.cleco.com
Central Reserve Life Corp./CRLC	Insurance/Life	6	def.	8.7%	X	0	17	B+	17800 Royalton Rd., Strongsville OH 44136 216/572-2400
Centura Banks Inc./CBC	Banking	53	19.6	2.0%	X	5	30	A	PO Box 1220, Rocky Mount NC 27802 800/436-5898 www.centura.com
Century Telephone Enter./CTL	Telephone	37	16.9	1.0%	X	7	23	A	PO Box 4065, Monroe LA 71211 800/833-1188 www.centurytel.com
Chemed Corp./CHE	Miscellaneous	36	12.7	5.8%	X	2	25	B+	255 E. Fifth St., Cincinnati OH 45202 800/224-3633

Company/Ticker	Industry								Address
Chemical Financial Corp./CHFC	Banking	34	15.2	2.5%	X	22	22	NA	PO Box 569, Midland MI 48640 517/839-5350
Chubb Corp./CB	Insurance/Prop.	67	22.0	1.7%	X	0	32	A–	PO Box 1615, Warren NJ 07061 908/902-2000 www.chubb.com
Cincinnati Financial Corp./CINF	Insurance/Prop.	81	17.8	2.0%	X	0	36	A	PO Box 145496, Cincinnati OH 53250 513/870-2639
Cintas Corp./CTAS	Special Services	70	36.6	0.4%		27	14	A+	PO Box 625737, Cincinnati OH 45262 513/459-1200
CIPSCO Inc./CIP	Electric Utility	37	16.9	5.7%	X	1	18	B+	607 E. Adams St., Springfield IL 62739 800/710-7726
Circuit City-Group/CC	Retail	36	26.9	0.4%		0	17	A	9950 Mayland Dr., Richmond VA 23233 804/527-4022 www.circuitcity.com
Cisco Systems Inc./CISCO	Computers	79	47.6	0.0%		10	0	B	PO Box 3075, Menlo Park CA 94026 800/553-6387 www.cisco.com
Citizens Banking Corp./CBCF	Banking	39	14.8	2.9%	X	14	13	A	328 S. Saginaw St., Flint MI 48502 810/257-2557
Citizens Utilities Co./CZNB	Electric Utility	8	10.8	0.0%		52	0	A+	High Ridge Park, Stanford CT 06905 800/248-8845 www.czn.net
CLARCOR Inc./CLC	Machinery	26	15.5	2.5%	X	4	36	B+	PO Box 7007, Rockford IL 61125 815/962-8867 www.clarcor.com
Clayton Homes Inc./CMH	Homebuilding	14	14.4	0.6%	X	16	1	B+	PO Box 15169, Knoxville TN 37901 423/595-4727 www.clayton.net.com

Company Name/ Stock Symbol	Industry	Price	P/E	YIELD	Dividend Reinvestment Plan	Year High EPS	Year High Dividend	S&P Rank	Address/Phone Number
Ciorox Co./CLX	Household Prods.	132	28.2	2.0%	X	6	20	A	PO Box 24305, Oakland CA 94623 510/271-2927 www.clorox.com
CNB Bancshares Inc./ BNK	Banking	42	19.6	2.1%	X(3)	2	14	A	PO Box 778, Evansville IN 47705 812/464-3400 www.citizensonline.com
Coca-Cola Co./KO	Soft Drink	70	45.2	0.8%	X	22	34	A+	One Coca-Cola Plaza, Atlanta GA 30313 800/633-0981 www.cocacola.com
Colgate-Palmolive Co./ CL	Household Prods.	74	36.5	1.5%	X	1	34	B+	300 Park Ave., New York NY 10022 213/310-3207 www.colgate.com
Colonial Gas Co./CGES	Natural Gas	22	11.5	6.1%	X(5)	2	17	B+	PO Box 3064, Lowell MA 01853 508/322-3000
Comerica Inc./CMA	Banking	72	19.6	2.4%	X	4	53	A−	PO Box 75000, Detroit MI 48275 800/292-1300 www.comerica.com
Commerce Bancshares Inc./CBSH	Banking	49	15.4	1.7%		10	28	A+	PO Box 13686, Kansas City MO 64199 816/234-2000 www.commercebank.com

Company/Symbol	Industry								Address
Compass Bancshares Inc./CBSS	Banking	35	16.2	2.7%	X	9	5	A	15 S. 20th St., Birmingham AL 35233 205/933-3331 www.compassweb.com
ConAgra Inc./CAG	Foods	67	25.0	1.6%	X	0	21	A+	One ConAgra Dr., Omaha NE 68102 800/840-3404
Connecticut Water Service/CTWS	Water Utility	29	12.8	5.9%	X	6	27	B+	93 W. Main St., Clinton CT 06413 860/669-8630
Consolidated Edison Co./ED	Electric Utility	31	11.3	6.8%	X	0	22	A	4 Irving Place, New York NY 10003 800/522-5522 www.coned.com
Consumers Water Co./CONW	Water Utility	17	15.9	7.1%	X	0	40	B	PO Box 599, Portland ME 04112 800/292-2925 www.consumerswater.com
Cooper Tire & Rubber Co./CTB	Auto Parts	24	16.8	1.4%		0	17	A	701 Lima Ave., Findlay OH 45840 419/423-1321
CoreStates Financial/CFL	Banking	59	15.9	2.8%	X	2	19	B+	PO Box 7618, Philadelphia, PA 19101 215/973-6006 www.CoreStates.com
Corus Bankshares Inc./CORS	Banking	29	9.6	1.7%		6	10	NA	3959 N. Lincoln Ave., Chicago IL 60613 773/549-7100
CPC International Inc./CPC	Foods	96	31.8	1.7%	X	2	11	A+	Intl. Plaza, Englewood Cliffs NJ 07632 201/894-4000 www.cpcinternational.com
Cracker Barrel Old Country/CBRL	Restaurant	25	19.1	0.1%	X	11	0	A	PO Box 787, Lebanon TN 37088 615/444-5533
Crawford & Co./CRDB	Insurance/Broker	18	21.4	2.4%		1	24	A	PO Box 5047, Atlanta GA 30302 404/256-0830 www.crawco.com

Company Name/ Stock Symbol	Industry	Price	P/E	YIELD	Dividend Reinvestment Plan	Year High EPS	Year High Dividend	S&P Rank	Address/Phone Number
CSX Corp./CSX	Transportation	57	14.5	1.8%	X	1	17	B+	PO Box 85629, Richmond VA 23285 804/782-1465 www.csx.com
Dayton Hudson Corp./ DH	Retail	57	24.1	1.1%	X	1	23	A	777 Nicollet Mall, Minneapolis MN 54402 612/370-6736
Dean Foods Co./DF	Foods	47	21.8	1.6%	X	0	22	B+	3600 N. River Rd., Franklin Park IL 60131 312/625-6200
Diebold Inc./DBD	Ofc. Equip./Supp.	45	28.5	1.1%	X	6	43	A	PO Box 3077, N. Canton OH 44720 800/766-5859 www.diebold.com
DiMon Inc./DMN	Tobacco	24	19.8	2.5%		1	22	NR	PO Box 681, Danville VA 24543 804/792-7511
Disney, Walt Co./DIS	Entertainment	78	28.4	0.7%	X	0	11	A	500 S. Buena Vista St., Burbank CA 91521 818/553-7200 www.disney.com
Dollar General Corp./ DG	Retail	41	38.3	0.5%		11	6	A+	104 Woodmont Blvd. #500, Nashville TN 37205 615/783-2000 www.dollargeneral.com
Donnelley, R.R & Sons Co./DNY	Printing	40	24.8	1.9%	X	0	25	B+	77 W. Wacker Dr., Chicago IL 60601 800/446-2617 www.donnelly.com

Company/Ticker	Industry								Address
Dover Corp./DOV	Machinery	70	18.4	1.0%		5	36	A	280 Park Ave., New York NY 10017 212/922-1640
Duke Energy Corp./DUK	Electric Utility	49	14.8	4.3%	X	4	21	A–	PO Box 1005, Charlotte NC 28201 800/488-3853 www.duke-energy.com
DuPont Co./DD	Chemicals	66	9.0	1.9%	X	3	4	B+	1007 Market St., Wilmington DE 19898 302/774-1000 www.dupont.com
Eaton Vance Corp./EV	Financial	29	15.3	1.4%		2	16	A–	24 Federal St., Boston MA 02110 617/482-8260
Electronic Data Systems/EDS	Computer Soft.	45	53.6	1.3%		0	34	A+	5400 Legacy Dr., Plano TX 75024 888/610-1122 www.eds.com
Emerson Electric Co./EMR	Electrical Equip.	57	24.2	1.9%	X	39	40	A+	PO Box 4100, St. Louis MO 63136 314/553-2197
Energen Corp./EGN	Natural Gas	35	13.6	3.5%	X	1	14	A	2101 Sixth Ave. N., Birmingham AL 35203 800/654-3206 www.energen.com
EnergyNorth Inc./EI	Natural Gas	22	12.2	5.8%	X	1	14	A–	PO Box 329, Manchester NH 03105 603/625-4000
Engelhard Corp./EC	Chemicals	22	19.8	1.6%	X	3	14	B+	101 Wood Ave., Iselin NJ 08830 908/205-6000
Ennis Business Forms Inc./EBF	Ofc. Equip./Supp.	9	12.9	6.9%		0	20	A–	107 N. Sherman St., Ennis TX 75-19 214/875-6581
Enova Corp./ENA	Electric Utility	24	13.1	6.5%	X	2	20	A–	PO Box 129400, San Diego CA 92112 800/826-5942 www.enova.com

Company Name/ Stock Symbol	Industry	Dividend Reinvestment Plan	Price	P/E	YIELD	Year High EPS	Year High Dividend	S&P Rank	Address/Phone Number
Equifax Inc./EFX	Special Services	X	31	23.0	1.1%	3	16	A–	PO Box 4081, Atlanta GA 30302 800/462-9853 www.equifax.com
Equitable of Iowa Cos./ EIC	Insurance	X	66	16.8	1.0%	9	10	A–	PO Box 1635, Des Moines IA 50306 800/369-5372
Exxon Corp./XON	Oil	X	63	19.5	2.6%	2	14	A–	PO Box 140369, Irving TX 75014 972/444-1156 www.exxon.com
F&M National Corp./ FMN	Banking	X	27	18.2	2.7%	2	10	A	38 Rouss Ave., Winchester VA 22601 540/665-4200
Family Dollar Stores Inc./FDO	Retail	X	29	35.8	1.1%	1	20	A–	PO Box 1017, Charlotte NC 28201 704/847-6961
Fannie Mae/FNM	Financial	X	43	16.7	2.0%	10	11	A	3900 Wisconsin Ave. NW, Washington DC 20016 800/366-2968 www.fanniemae.com
Fastenal Corp./FAST	Retail		55	57.9	0.0%	14	0	A–	2001 Theurer Blvd., Winona MN 55987 507/454-5374
Federal Realty Inv. Trust/FRT	RE Invest. Trust	X	27	13.6	6.2%	4	29	NA	1626 E. Jefferson St., Rockville MD 20852 800/658-8980

Company/Ticker	Industry								Address
Fifth Third Bancorp/ FITB	Banking	61	26.8	1.4%	X	23	23	A+	Fifth Third Ctr., Cincinnati OH 45263 513/579/5300 www.53.com
First Chicago NBD Corp./FCN	Banking	67	14.7	2.1%	X	1	30	B –	Mail Suite 0460, Chicago, IL 60670 312/732-4812 www.fcnbd.com
First Commerce Bancshares/FCBIA	Banking	23	13.2	1.3%	X	1	12	NA	1248 O St., Lincoln NE 68508 402/434-4110 www.fcbi.com
First Commercial Corp./ FCLR	Banking	42	17.1	2.3%	X	10	10	A+	400 W. Capitol Ave., Little Rock AR 72201 501/371-7000 www.firstcommercial.com
First Empire State Corp./FES(A)	Banking	350	15.5	0.9%	X	14	16	A+	PO Box 223, Buffalo NY 14240 716/842-5445
First Merchants Corp./ FRME	Banking	31	15.3	3.1%	X	21	14	A+	PO Box 792, Muncie IN 47308 800/262-4261 www.firstmerchants.com
FirstMerit Corp./FMER	Banking	48	19.0	2.4%	X	1	15	A –	III Cascade Plaza, Akron OH 44308 330/996-6300
First Northern Capital Corp./FNGB	Banking	25	31.2	2.6%	X	0	12	B +	PO Box 23100, Green Bay WI 54305 800/999-3675
First of America Bank Corp./FOA	Banking	52	26.9	1.6%	X(5)	2	14	A –	211 S. Rose St., Kalamazoo MI 49007 616/376-9000 www.first-of-america.com
First Tennessee National/FTEN	Banking	49	17.4	2.4%	X	7	19	A	PO Box 84, Memphis TN 38101 90*/523-5620 www.ftb.com
First Union Corp./FTU	Banking	48	15.0	2.7%	X(1)	7	19	A –	Two First Union Ctr., Charlotte NC 28288 704/374-6782 www.firstunion.com

Company Name/Stock Symbol	Industry	Price	P/E	YIELD	Dividend Reinvestment Plan	Year High EPS	Year High Dividend	S&P Rank	Address/Phone Number
First Virginia Banks Inc./FVB	Banking	66	18.0	2.4%	X	1	20	A	PO Box 88, Falls Church VA 22040 703/241-4000 www.firstvirginia.com
Firstar Corp./FSR	Banking	33	17.0	2.5%	X	7	18	A−	PO Box 2077, Milwaukee WI 53201 414/765-4321 www.firstar.com
Fleetwood Enterprises/FLE	Homebuilding	30	13.0	2.3%	X	1	14	B+	PO Box 7638, Riverside CA 92513 909/351-3500 www.fleetwood.com
Florida Progress Corp./FPC	Electric Utility	32	21.1	6.6%	X	4	44	A−	PO Box 33028, St. Petersburg FL 33733 800/352-1121 www.fpc.com
Flowers Industries Inc./FLO	Foods	18	29.0	2.4%	X	0	24	B	PO Box 1338, Thomasville GA 31799 912/226-9110
Franklin Resources Inc./BEN	Investment Bank	80	28.4	0.5%	X	17	16	A+	777 Mariners Island Blvd., San Mateo CA 94404 800/342-5236
Fremont General Corp./FMT	Insurance/Prop.	41	12.6	1.5%		3	10	A−	2020 Santa Monica Blvd., Santa Monica CA 90404 310/315-5500
Frisch's Restaurants Inc./FRS(A)	Restaurant	16	NMF	1.5%		0	22	B+	2800 Gilbert Ave., Cincinnati OH 45206 513/961-2660

Company/Symbol	Industry							Address
Frontier Corp./FRO	Telephone	20	23.8	4.3%	X	0	B+	180 S. Clinton Ave., Rochester NY 14646 800/836-0342 www.frontiercorp.com
Fuller, H.B. Co./FULL	Chemicals	49	13.5	1.5%	X(3)	3	A–	PO Box 64683, St. Paul MN 55164 800/214-2523
Fulton Financial Corp./FULT	Banking	27	18.1	2.3%	X	15	NA	PO Box 4887, Lancaster PA 17604 800/626-0255 www.fult.com
Gallagher, Arthur J. & Co./AJG	Insurance/Broker	36	12.0	3.4%	X	5	A–	Two Pierce Place, Itasca IL 60143 630/773-3800 www.ajg.com
Gannett Co. Inc./GCI	Publishing	104	23.1	1.4%	X	5	A	1100 Wilson Blvd., Arlington VA 22234 703/284-6000 www.gannett.com
GATX Corp./GMT	Transportation	62	14.2	3.0%	X	4	A–	500 W. Monroe, Chicago IL 60661 800/428-8161 www.gatx.com
General Binding Corp./GBND	Ofc. Equip./Supp.	27	16.0	1.6%	X	3	B+	One GBC Plaza, Northbrook IL 60062 847/272-3700
General Electric Co./GE	Electrical Equip.	72	30.8	1.4%	X	21	A+	Fairfield CT 06431 800/786-2543 www.ge.com
General Re Corp./GRN	Insurance/Prop.	194	17.5	1.1%	X	2	A	PO Box 10351, Stamford CT 06904 203/328-5000
Genovese Drug Stores/GDXA(A)	Retail Drug	19	22.4	1.5%		1	A–	80 Marcus Dr., Melville NY 11747 515/420-1900
Genuine Parts Co./GPC	Auto Parts	34	18.1	2.8%	X	14	A+	2999 Circle 75 Pkwy., Atlanta GA 30339 770/953-1700

Company Name/Stock Symbol	Industry	Price	P/E	YIELD	Dividend Reinvestment Plan	Year High EPS	Year High Dividend	S&P Rank	Address/Phone Number
Giant Food Inc./GFSA(A)	Grocery	33	26.4	2.4%	X	0	25	B+	PO Box 1804, Washington DC 20013 301/341-8480 www.cgonews.com/gfs
Gillette Co./G	Cosmetics	100	54.3	0.9%	X	0	19	A+	Prudential Tower, Boston MA 02199 617/421-7000
Glacier Bancorp Inc./GBCI	Banking	19	17.3	2.5%	X	0	10	A+	PO Box 27, Kalispell MT 55903 406/756-4200 www.glacierbank.com
Golden Enterprises Inc./GLDC	Foods	7	24.1	6.9%		0	25	B	2101 Magnolia Ave. So. #212, Birmingham AL 35205 205/326-6101
Golden West Financial/GDW	Savings & Loan	77	11.6	0.6%		1	14	A−	1901 Harrison St., Oakland CA 94612 415/446-3420
Gorman-Rupp Co./GRC(A)	Manufacturing	18	12.3	3.1%	X	10	24	A−	PO Box 1217, Mansfield OH 44901 419/755-1011
Graco Inc./GGG	Manufacturing	33	15.5	1.7%	X	3	11	A−	PO Box 1441, Minneapolis MN 55440 612/623-6778
Grainger, W.W. Inc./GWW	Electrical Equip.	96	22.5	1.1%		2	25	A	455 Knightsbridge Pkwy., Lincolnshire IL 60069 847/793-9030 www.grainger.com

Company/Ticker	Industry								Address
Great Lakes Chemical Corp./GLK	Chemicals	48	13.3	1.3%		A+	0	23	One Great Lakes Blvd., W. Lafayette IN 47906 317/497-6100
Grey Advertising Inc./GREY	Special Services	324	16.8	1.2%		B	2	22	777 Third Ave., New York NY 10017 212/546-2000
Hach Co./HACH	Waste Management	21	19.1	1.1%		A	13	15	PO Box 389, Loveland CO 80539 970/669-3050
Hannaford Brothers Co./HRD	Grocery	33	18.2	1.6%	X	A+	17	34	PO Box 1000, Portland ME 04104 207/883-2911 www.hannaford.com/shop
Harcourt General Inc./H	Publishing	47	18.9	1.5%	X	B+	2	28	27 Boylston St., Chestnut Hill MA 02167 800/225-9194 www.irin.com/H.
Harleysville Group Inc./HGIC	Insurance/Prop.	37	13.4	2.3%	X	B+	0	10	355 Maple Ave., Harleysville PA 19438 215/256-5151 www.harleysvillegroup.com
Harleysville National Corp./HNBC	Banking	35	15.7	2.3%	X	NA	21	22	PO Box 195, Harleysville PA 19438 800/423-3955
Hasbro Inc./HAS(A)	Toys	29	18.4	0.9%	X	A−	1	18	PO Box 1059, Pawtucket RI 02862 401/431-8697 www.hasbro.com
Haverty Furniture Cos. Inc./HAVT	Household Furn.	14	12.3	2.3%		B	1	21	866 W. Peachtree St. NW, Atlanta GA 30308 404/881-1911
Hawaiian Electric Industries/HE	Electric Utility	37	29.1	6.5%	X	B+	0	33	PO Box 730, Honolulu HI 96808 808/543-7385 www.hei.com
HealthCare COMPARE Corp./HCCC	Health Care	55	23.7	0.0%		B+	14	0	3200 Highland Ave., Downers Grove IL 60515 630/241-7900

Company Name/Stock Symbol	Industry	Price	P/E	YIELD	Dividend Reinvestment Plan	Year High EPS	Year High Dividend	S&P Rank	Address/Phone Number
Health Care Property Investors/HC	RE Invest. Trust	36	12.7	6.7%		11	11	NA	10990 Wilshire Blvd. #1200, Los Angeles CA 90024 310/444-7817
Heilig-Meyers Co./HMY	Household Furn.	17	21.2	1.6%	X	0	21	A	2235 Staples Mill Rd., Richmond VA 23230 804/359-9171 www.heiligmeyers.com
Heinz, H.J. Co./HNZ	Foods	46	56.8	2.5%	X	0	30	A	PO Box 57, Pittsburgh PA 15230 800/253-3399 www.hjheinz.com
Helmerich & Payne Inc./HP	Oil & Gas Drill.	66	28.2	0.8%		1	25	B	Utica at 21st St., Tulsa OK 74114 918/742-5531
Hershey Foods Corp./HSY	Foods	55	29.9	1.5%	X	2	22	A	PO Box 810, Hershey PA 17033 717/534-7556 www.hersheys.com
Hewlett-Packard Co./HWP	Computers	66	25.0	0.8%		5	10	A	3000 Hanover St., Palo Alto CA 94304 415/857-1501 www.hp.com
Hillenbrand Industries Inc./HB	Manufacturing	47	22.6	1.4%	X	2	24	A	700 State Rte. 46 E., Batesville IN 47006 812/934-8400 www.hillenbrand.com

Company/Ticker	Sector								Address
Home Depot Inc./HD	Retail	47	34.3	0.4%	X	11	9	A+	2455 Paces Ferry Rd., Atlanta GA 30339 770/384-3456 www.homedepot.com
HON Industries Inc./HONI	Ofc. Equip./Supp.	58	23.4	1.0%		1	12	A−	PO Box 1109, Muscatine IA 52761 319/264-7400
Honeywell Inc./HON	Electrical Equip.	77	22.8	1.4%	X	3	21	B+	PO Box 524, Minneapolis MN 55440 612/951-2122 www.honeywell.com
Hormel Foods Corp./HRL	Foods	28	26.7	2.2%	X	0	30	A	1 Hormel Place, Austin MN 55912 507/437-5669
Houghton Mifflin Co./HTN	Publishing	68	23.9	1.5%	X	1	14	B+	222 Berkeley St., Boston MA 02116 617/351-5000 www.hmco.com
Household International Inc./HI	Financial	118	21.4	1.3%	X(2)	5	44	B+	2700 Sanders Rd., Prospect Heights IL 60070 847/564-7369
HSB Group/HSB	Insurance/Prop.	54	20.8	4.2%	X	0	31	B	PO Box 5024, Hartford CT 06102 860/722-5180
Hubbell Inc./HUBB	Electrical Equip.	49	22.0	2.1%	X	3	36	A	PO Box 549, Orange CT 06477 203/799-4100
Huntington Banchshares/HBAN	Banking	28	16.2	2.6%	X	6	30	A	PO Box 1558, Columbus OH 43272 614/480-3803 www.huntington.com
IKON Office Solutions Inc./IKN	Ofc. Equip./Supp.	26	27.1	2.2%	X	3	32	B+	Box 834, Valley Forge PA 19482 610/993-3526 www.IKON.com
Illinois Tool Works Inc./ITW	Manufacturing	54	25.1	0.9%	X	5	34	A+	3600 W. Lake Ave., Glenview IL 60025 847/724-7500

Company Name/ Stock Symbol	Industry	Price	P/E	YIELD	Dividend Reinvestment Plan	Year High EPS	Year High Dividend	S&P Rank	Address/Phone Number
Indiana Energy Inc./IEI	Natural Gas	24	14.0	4.6%	X	1	24	A−	1630 N. Meridian St., Indianapolis IN 46202 800/777-3389
International Dairy Queen/INDQA	Restaurant	25	15.1	0.0%		23	0	B+	7505 Metro Blvd., Minneapolis MN 55439 800/488-8444
Intl. Flavors & Fragrances/IFF	Cosmetics	51	30.2	2.8%	X	0	35	A	521 W. 57th St., New York NY 10019 212/765-5500
Interpublic Group of Cos./IPG	Special Services	42	25.1	1.3%	X	2	13	A+	1271 Ave. of the Americas, New York NY 10020 212/399-8000
Ionics Inc./ION	Manufacturing	42	24.7	0.0%		10	0	B+	PO Box 9131, Watertown MA 02272 617/926-2500 www.ionics.com
Jefferson-Pilot Corp./JP	Insurance/Life	71	15.3	2.3%	X	9	28	A+	PO Box 21008, Greensboro NC 27420 910/691-3000 www.jpc.com
Johnson & Johnson/JNJ	Health Care	63	26.9	1.4%	X	38	34	A+	New Brunswick NJ 08933 800/950-5089 www.jnj.com
Johnson Controls Inc./ JCI	Manufacturing	43	16.7	2.0%	X	6	21	A−	PO Box 591, Milwaukee WI 53201 414/228-2363 www.jci.com

Company/Symbol	Industry								Address
Kansas City Power & Light/KLT	Electric Utility	29	29.3	5.6%	X	0	10	A−	120 Walnut, Kansas City MO 64106 816/556-2312 www.kcpl.com
Kaydon Corp./KDN	Machinery	60	18.1	0.9%		4	10	A	19345 UW 19 N., Clearwater FL 34624 813/531-1101
Keane Inc./KEA(A)	Special Services	63	NMF	0.0%		10	0	B+	Ten City Sq., Boston MA 02129 617/241-9200 www.keane.com
Kellogg Co./K	Foods	88	38.1	1.8%	X	1	40	A	PO Box CAMB, Battle Creek MI 49016 800/962-1413 www.kelloggs.com
Kelly Services Inc./KELYA	Special Services	31	15.9	2.8%		5	25	A	999 W. Big Beaver Rd., Troy MI 48084 810/362-4444 www.kellyservices.com
Kenan Transport Co./KTCO	Transportation	20	12.8	1.4%		1	18	NA	PO Box 2729, Chapel Hill NC 27515 919/967-8221
KeyCorp/KEY	Banking	59	16.6	2.8%	X	9	16	A+	127 Public Square, Cleveland OH 44114 800/539-7216 www.keybank.com
Keystone Financial Inc./KSTN	Banking	34	19.7	3.1%	X	8	12	A−	PO Box 708, Altoona PA 16603 814/946-6691 www.keyfin.com
Kimball International Inc./KBALB	Household Furn.	41	14.9	2.8%		3	25	A−	1600 Royal St., Jasper IN 47549 812/482-1600
Kimberly-Clark Corp./KMB	Household Prods.	49	20.0	2.0%	X	1	23	A	Box 612606, Dallas TX 75261 800/639-1352 www.kimberly-clark.com

Company Name/Stock Symbol	Industry	Price	P/E	YIELD	Dividend Reinvestment Plan	Year High EPS	Year High Dividend	S&P Rank	Address/Phone Number
KU Energy Corp./KU	Electric Utility	33	16.3	5.3%	X	2	15	A	One Quality St., Lexington KY 40507 800/786-2558
Lancaster Colony Corp./LANC	Foods	53	19.1	1.4%	X	6	34	A	37 W. Broad St., Columbus OH 43215 614/224-7141
La-Z-Boy Inc./LZB	Household Furn.	37	14.8	2.3%	X	6	16	A−	1284 N. Telegraph Rd., Monroe MI 48162 313/241-4414 www.lazboy.com
Lee Enterprises Inc./LEE	Publishing	25	18.8	2.1%		5	36	A−	215 N. Main St., Davenport IA 52801 319/383-2100
Legg Mason Inc./LM	Investment Bank	56	18.7	0.9%		3	15	A−	PO Box 1476, Baltimore MD 21203 410/539-0000
Leggett & Platt Inc./LEG	Household Furn.	44	21.8	1.2%		6	25	A	No. 1 Leggett Rd., Carthage MO 64836 417/358-8131
LG&E Energy Corp./LGE	Electric Utility	22	14.9	5.2%	X	2	42	B+	PO Box 32030, Louisville KY 40232 800/235-9705 www.lgeenergy.com
Lilly, Eli & Co./LLY	Health Care	114	39.9	1.3%	X	3	29	A	PO Box 88665, Indianapolis IN 46208 800/833-8699 www.lilly.com
Lilly Industries Inc./LI	Bldng. Materials	22	25.6	1.5%	X	0	16	B+	733 S.W. St., Indianapolis IN 46225 317/687-6700

Company/Ticker	Industry								Address
Lincoln National Corp./LNC	Insurance/Life	66	19.3	3.0%	X	2	13	A–	PO Box 7845, Ft. Wayne IN 46801 800/237-2920 www.lnc.com
Linear Technology Corp./LLTC	Electronics	58	33.9	0.3%	X	11	4	B+	1630 McCarthy Blvd., Milpitas CA 95035 408/432-1900 www.linear-tech.com
Lockheed Martin Corp./LMT	Aerospace/Def.	102	14.6	1.6%	X	5	25	NA	6801 Rockledge Dr., Bethesda MD 20817 301/897-6000 www.lmco.com
Louisiana-Pacific Corp./LPX	Paper/Forest	23	def.	2.4%	X	0	20	B	111 SW Fifth Ave., Portland OR 97204 503/221-0800 www.lpx.com
Lowe's Companies Inc./LOW	Retail	36	19.6	0.6%	X	1	16	A–	PO Box 1111, N. Wilkesboro NC 28656 910/658-4385 www.lowes.com
Lubrizol Corp./LZ	Chemicals	44	18.0	2.3%	X	1	13	B+	29400 Lakeland Blvd., Wickliffe OH 44092 216/943-4200 www.lubrizol.com
Luby's Cafeterias Inc./LUB	Restaurant	20	12.5	4.0%	X	29	31	A	PO Box 33069, San Antonio TX 78265 210/654-9000
Madison Gas & Electric Co./MDSN	Electric Utility	20	45.5	6.4%	X	0	16	B+	PO Box 1231, Madison WI 53701 800/356-6423 www.mge.com
Marcus Corp./MCS	Hotel/Motel	24	31.6	1.3%	X	8	12	A	250 E. Wisconsin Ave. #1700, Milwaukee WI 53202 414/272-6020
Marsh & McClennan Cos./MMC	Insurance Broker	72	21.2	2.8%	X	12	36	A+	1166 Ave. of Americas, New York NY 10036 212/345-5475

Company Name/Stock Symbol	Industry	Dividend Reinvestment Plan	Price	P/E	YIELD	Year High EPS	Year High Dividend	S&P Rank	Address/Phone Number
Marshall & Ilsley Corp./MRIS	Banking	X	42	19.1	1.9%	2	24	A–	770 N. Water St., Milwaukee WI 53202 414/765-7801 www.micorp.com
Masco Corp./MAS	Bldng. Materials		42	24.4	1.9%	2	38	B	21001 Van Born Rd., Taylor MI 48180 313/274-7400 www.masco.com
May Department Stores Co./MAY	Retail	X	52	18.3	2.3%	22	22	A+	611 Olive St., St. Louis MO 63101 314/342-6300 www.maycompany.com
MBIA Inc./MBI	Financial		115	15.5	1.3%	10	9	A+	113 King St., Armonk NY 10504 914/765-3014 www.mbia.com
McClatchy Newspapers Inc./MNI	Publishing		34	22.4	1.1%	1	13	B+	PO Box 15779, Sacramento CA 95852 916/321-1846
McCormick & Co. Inc./MCCRK	Foods	X	25	40.3	2.4%	0	10	A–	18 Loveton Cir., Sparks MD 21152 800/424-5855 www.mccormick.com
McDonald's Corp./MCD	Restaurant	X	51	22.0	0.6%	32	22	A+	McDonald's Plaza, Oak Brook IL 60521 630/623-7428 www.mcdonalds.com
McGraw-Hill Companies Inc./MHP	Publishing	X	66	27.3	2.2%	3	22	NA	1221 Ave. of Americas, New York NY 10020 212/512-2000 www.mcgraw-hill.com

Company/Ticker	Industry								Address
Meditrust/MT	RE Invest. Trust	40	13.1	7.0%	X	4	11	NA	197 First Ave., Needham MA 02194 617/433-6000 www.reit.com
Medtronic Inc./MDT	Medical Prods.	92	41.4	0.5%	X	14	19	A+	7000 Central Ave. NE, Minneapolis MN 55432 612/574-3035 www.medtronic.com
Mercantile Bankshares/MRBK	Banking	29	16.6	2.8%	X(5)	21	20	A	PO Box 1477, Baltimore MD 21203 410/237-5900
Merck & Co. Inc./MRK	Health Care	106	30.1	1.7%	X	3	21	A+	PO Box 100-WS3AB-40, Whitehouse Station NJ 08889 800/613-2104 www.merck.com
Mercury General Corp./MCY	Insurance/Multi	76	9.7	1.5%		2	10	A–	4484 Wilshire Blvd., Los Angeles CA 90010 800/900-6729
Microsoft Corp./MSFT	Computer Soft.	144	54.8	0.0%		21	0	B+	One Microsoft Way, Redmond WA 98052 800/285-7772 www.microsoft.com
Middlesex Water Co./MSEX	Water Utility	17	13.8	6.6%	X	0	23	A–	PO Box 1500, Iselin NJ 08830 908/634-1500
Midland Co./MLA(A)	Insurance/Multi	52	12.6	1.3%		0	10	A–	PO Box 1256, Cincinnati OH 45201 513/943-7100
Millipore Corp./MIL	Manufacturing	43	def.	0.8%	X	0	26	B+	80 Ashby Rd., Bedford MA 01730 617/533-2032 www.millipore.com
Mine Safety Appliances Co./MNES	Health Care	63	14.3	2.0%		3	26	B+	121 Gamma Dr., O'Hara Township, Pittsburgh PA 15238 412/967-3000

Company Name/ Stock Symbol	Industry	Price	P/E	YIELD	Dividend Reinvestment Plan	Year High EPS	Year High Dividend	S&P Rank	Address/Phone Number
Minnesota Mining & Mfg./MMM	Manufacturing	100	26.0	2.1%	X	5	38	A+	3M Ctr. 216-2N-10, St. Paul MN 55144 612/733-3564 www.mmm.com
Mobile Gas Service Corp./MBLE	Natural Gas	29	11.2	4.1%	X	1	20	B+	PO Box 2248, Mobile AL 36652 334/450-4638
Modine Manufacturing Co./MODI	Auto Parts	30	13.9	2.5%	X	1	13	A	1500 DeKoven Ave., Racine WI 53403 414/636-1361
Monsanto Co./MTC	Chemicals	51	NMF	1.3%	X	0	24	B+	800 N. Lindbergh Blvd., St. Louis MO 63167 314/694-5432 www.monsanto.com
Morgan, J.P. & Co. Inc./JPM	Banking	108	14.9	3.3%	X	2	20	B+	60 Wall St., New York NY 10260 212/648-9446 www.jpmorgan.com
Myers Industries Inc./MYE(A)	Manufacturing	16	13.3	1.2%	X	1	22	A	1293 S. Main St., Akron OH 44301 330/253-5592
NACCO Industries/NC	Machinery	62	12.8	1.3%	X	0	18	B	5875 Landerbrook Dr., Mayfield Heights OH 44124 216/449-9600
Nash Finch Co./NAFC	Distributors	21	11.5	3.6%	X	3	28	A-	PO Box 355, Minneapolis MN 55440 612/832-0534

Company/Symbol	Industry							Grade	Address
National Commerce Bancorp./NCBC	Banking	24	19.2	1.8%	X	19	22	A	One Commerce Sq., Memphis TN 38150 901/523-3434 www.ncbcorp.com
National Fuel Gas Co./NFG	Natural Gas	41	13.9	4.1%	X	1	25	B+	10 Lafayette Sq., Buffalo NY 14203 716/857-7070 www.natfuel.com
National Penn Bancshares/NPBC	Banking	34	20.2	2.5%	X	19	8	NA	PO Box 547, Boyertown PA 19512 610/369-6291 www.natpennbank.com
National Sanitary Supply Co./NSSX	Miscellaneous	14	18.2	2.3%		0	10	NA	255 E. Fifth St., Cincinnati OH 45202 513/762-6500
National Security Group/NSEC	Insurance/Multi.	14	14.0	4.9%	X	1	19	B+	661 E. Davis St., Elba AL 36323 334/897-2273
National Service Industries/NSI	Special Services	49	21.4	2.4%	X	5	35	A	1420 Peachtree St. NE, Atlanta GA 30309 404/853-1216
NationsBank Corp./NB	Banking	68	15.9	1.9%	X	5	19	A−	Charlotte NC 28255 800/521-3984 www.NationsBank.com
Newell Co./NWL	Housewares	42	24.6	1.5%	X	14	4	A+	29 E. Stephenson St., Freeport IL 61032 815/235-4171 www.newellco.com
New Plan Reality Trust/NPR	RE Invest. Trust	23	15.2	6.3%	X(5)	4	21	NA	1120 Ave. of Americas, New York NY 10036 212/869-3000
Nordson Corp./NDSN	Machinery	61	22.8	1.3%	X	6	33	A	28601 Clemens Rd., Westlake OH 44145 216/892-1580 www.nordson.com
Norfolk Southern Corp./NSC	Railroad	113	19.7	2.1%	X	3	10	A+	Three Commercial Place, Norfolk VA 23510 757/629-2600 www.nscorp.com

Company Name/Stock Symbol	Industry	Price	P/E	YIELD	Dividend Reinvestment Plan	Year High EPS	Year High Dividend	S&P Rank	Address/Phone Number
North Carolina Natural Gas/NCG	Natural Gas	34	12.5	4.1%	X(5)		2	18	A–	PO Box 909, Fayetteville NC 28302 910/483-0315
Northern States Power Co./NSP	Electric Utility	51	14.9	5.5%	X		0	22	A–	414 Nicollet Mall, Minneapolis MN 55401 800/527-4677 www.nspco.com
Northern Trust Corp./NTRS	Banking	54	22.4	1.3%			9	10	A	50 S. La Salle St., Chicago IL 60675 312/444-7811 www.ntrs.com
Northwest Natural Gas Co./NWNG	Natural Gas	27	13.4	4.4%	X		1	41	B+	220 NW 2nd Ave., Portland OR 97209 800/422-4012 www.nng.com
Northwestern Public Service/NPS	Electric Utility	19	16.8	4.6%	X		4	14	A	PO Box 1318, Huron SD 57350 800/677-6716 www.northwestern.com
Nucor Corp./NUE	Steel	58	18.3	0.7%	X		0	24	A–	2100 Rexford Rd., Charlotte NC 28211 704/366-7000
Ohio Casualty Corp./OCAS	Insurance/Prop.	45	10.4	3.7%	X		3	50	B+	136 N. Third St., Hamilton OH 45025 513/867-3000 www.ocas.com
Old Kent Financial Corp./OKEN	Banking	55	15.1	2.4%	X		37	38	A+	111 Lyon St. NW, Grand Rapids MI 49503 800/652-2657

Company	Industry								Address
Old National Bancorp/OLDB	Banking	44	19.0	2.1%	X(3)	1	10	A–	420 Main St., Evansville IN 47708 812/464-1266 www.oldnational.com
Old Republic International/ORI	Insurance/Multi.	31	12.3	1.7%	X	2	15	A–	307 N. Michigan Ave., Chicago IL 60601 312/346-8100
One Valley Bancorp Inc./OV	Banking	43	17.5	2.2%	X	14	15	NA	PO Box 1793, Charleston WV 25326 304/348-7023
Orange & Rockland Utilities/ORU	Electric Utility	33	12.6	7.8%	X	2	21	A–	PO Box 3006, Pearl River NY 10955 914/577-2512
Osmonics Inc./OSM	Waste Mgmt.	18	20.0	0.0%		10	0	B+	5951 Clearwater Dr., Minnetonka MN 55343 612/933-2277 www.osmonics.com
Otter Tail Power Co./OTTR	Electric Utility	33	13.4	5.6%	X	9	21	A–	PO Box 496, Fergus Falls MN 56538 800/664-1259
Pacific Century Financial/BOH	Banking	48	14.5	2.5%	X	2	18	A	PO Box 2900, Honolulu HI 96846 808/537-8037 www.boh.com/econ
Pall Corp./PLL	Manufacturing	24	34.8	2.3%	X	3	22	A	2200 Northern Blvd., East Hills NY 11548 800/205-7255 www.pall.com
Park National Corp./PRK(A)	Banking	76	19.6	2.1%	X	36	36	A–	PO Box 3500, Newark OH 43058 614/349-3708
Parker Hannifin Corp./PH	Manufacturing	62	18.7	1.5%	X	2	40	B+	17325 Euclid Ave., Cleveland OH 44112 216/531-3000 www.parker.com
Pentair Inc./PNR	Manufacturing	37	19.7	1.5%	X	6	20	A–	1500 County Rd. B2 W., St. Paul MN 55113 612/636-7920

Company Name/Stock Symbol	Industry	Price	P/E	YIELD	Dividend Reinvestment Plan	Year High EPS	Year High Dividend	S&P Rank	Address/Phone Number
Peoples-Bancorp Inc./PEBO	Banking	38	17.2	1.9%		23	31	NA	PO Box 738, Marietta OH 45750 614/374-6136 www.peoplesbancorp.com
Peoples Energy Corp./PGL	Natural Gas	38	12.5	4.9%	X	1	13	B+	PO Box 2000, Chicago IL 60690 800/228-6888 www.pecorp.com
Pep Boys-Manny, Moe & Jack/PBY	Retail	34	20.5	0.7%	X	7	20	A+	3111 W. Allegheny Ave., Philadelphia PA 19132 800/737-2697 www.pepboys.com
PepsiCo Inc./PEP	Soft Drink	38	NMF	1.3%	X	0	24	A	Purchase NY 10577 914/253-3055 www.pepsico.com
Pfizer Inc./PFE	Health Care	61	39.1	1.1%	X	3	29	A−	235 E. 42nd St., New York NY 10017 212/573-2323 www.pfizer.com
Philip Morris Cos. Inc./MO	Tobacco	43	15.6	3.7%	X	3	31	A+	120 Park Ave., New York NY 10017 800/367-5415
Piedmont Natural Gas Co./PNY	Natural Gas	25	14.3	4.9%	X(5)	2	18	A−	PO Box 33068, Charlotte NC 28233 704/364-3120 www.piedmontng.com
Pitney Bowes Inc./PBI	Ofc. Equip./Supp.	74	22.9	2.2%	X	15	14	A+	1 Elmcroft Rd., Stamford CT 06926 203/356-5000 www.pitneybowes.com

Company/Symbol	Industry								Address
Potlatch Corp./PCH	Paper/Forest	47	24.9	3.5%	X	0	13	B	PO Box 193591, San Francisco CA 94119 415/576-8800
PPG Industries Inc./PPG	Chemicals	62	15.6	2.1%	X	3	15	A–	One PPG Place, Pittsburgh PA 15222 412/434-3312 www.ppg.com
Procter & Gamble Co./PG	Household Prods.	152	33.9	1.3%	X	3	41	A	PO Box 559, Cincinnati OH 45201 800/742-6253 www.pg.com
Progressive Corp./PGR	Insurance/Prop.	97	20.7	0.2%		1	27	B+	6300 Wilson Mills Rd., Mayfield Village OH 44143 216/446-2851 www.auto-insurance.com
Providian Financial Corp./PVN	Insurance/Life	34	20.4	0.0%	X	27	34	A	PO Box 32830, Louisville KY 40232 502/560-2391 www.providian.com
Public Service Co. of NC/PGS	Natural Gas	20	14.7	4.6%	X	3	26	B+	PO Box 1398, Gastonia NC 28053 800/784-6443
Quaker Chemical Corp./KWR	Chemicals	17	def.	4.1%		0	25	B–	Conshohocken PA 19428 610/832-4119
Questar Corp./STR	Natural Gas	41	16.1	3.0%	X	1	18	A	PO Box 45433, Salt Lake City UT 84-45 800/729-6788 www.questarcorp.com
Raven Industries Inc./RAVN	Textiles	24	14.4	2.2%		2	10	B+	Box 5107, Sioux Falls SD 57117 605/336-2750
Raymond James Financial Inc./RJF	Investment Bank	27	11.5	1.2%		2	11	A–	880 Carillon Pkwy., St. Petersburg FL 33716 813/573-3800 www.rjf.com

Company Name/Stock Symbol	Industry	Price	P/E	YIELD	Dividend Reinvestment Plan	Year High EPS	Year High Dividend	S&P Rank	Address/Phone Number
Raytheon Co./RTN	Aerospace/Def.	55	17.1	1.5%	X	0	13	A+	141 Spring St., Lexington MA 02173 617/860-2303 www.raytheon.com
Reader's Digest Association/RDA	Publishing	26	13.3	3.5%	X	0	10	B+	Pleasantville NY 10570 914/244-7615 www.readersdigest.com
Regions Financial Corp./RGBK	Banking	34	17.0	2.4%	X	25	25	A+	PO Box 10247, Birmingham AL 35202 334/832-8493 www.regionsbank.com
ReliaStar Financial Corp./RLR	Insurance/Life	77	16.0	1.6%	X	5	25	A	20 Washington Ave. S., Minneapolis MN 55401 612/372-5574 www.reliastar.com
Republic New York Corp./RNB	Banking	110	14.8	1.7%	X	1	31	B+	452 Fifth Ave., New York NY 10018 212/525-6225 www.rnb.com
RLI Corp./RLI	Insurance/Prop.	38	12.0	1.6%	X	2	20	B+	9025 N. Lindbergh Dr., Peoria IL 61615 800/331-4929 www.rlicorp.com
Rockwell International Corp./ROK	Aerospace	65	23.3	1.8%	X	4	20	A−	PO Box 4250, Seal Beach CA 90740 310/797-5986 www.rockwell.com

Company/Symbol	Industry								Address
Rohm & Haas Co./ROH	Chemicals	93	5.6	2.2%		3	9	B+	100 Independence Mall W., Philadelphia PA 19106 215/592-3045 www.rohmhaas.com
Rollins Inc./ROL	Special Services	19	29.7	3.2%	X	0	11	B+	2170 Piedmont Rd. NE, Atlanta GA 30324 404/888-2000
RPM Inc./RPOW	Chemicals	19	20.0	2.5%	X	49	23	A+	PO Box 777, Medina OH 44258 330/273-5090
Rubbermaid Inc./RBD	Housewares	26	26.5	2.3%	X	1	43	A	1147 Akron Rd., Wooster OH 44691 330/264-6464 www.rubbermaid.com
Ruddick Corp./RDK	Grocery/Textile	15	14.7	2.1%	X	2	11	B+	2000 Two First Union Ctr., Charlotte NC 28282 704/372-5404
SAFECO Corp./SAFC	Insurance/Prop.	46	13.2	2.8%		2	25	A−	SAFECO Plaza, Seattle WA 98185 206/545-5000 www.safeco.com
St. Joseph Light & Power Co./SAJ	Electric Utility	16	13.0	6.0%	X	0	16	A−	PO Box 998, St. Joseph MO 64502 800/367-4562
St. Paul Companies/SPC	Insurance/Prop.	80	11.4	2.3%	X	4	11	A−	385 Washington St., St. Paul MN 55102 612/310-7911 www.stpaul.com
Sallie Mae/SLM	Financial	139	18.0	1.2%		23	20	A	1050 Thomas Jefferson St. NW, Washington DC 20007 202/333-8000 www.salliemae.com
Sara Lee Corp./SLE	Foods	44	22.8	1.9%	X	2	20	A	Three First Natl. Plaza, Chicago IL 60602 312/558-8662
SBC Communications Inc./SBC	Telephone	59	16.7	2.9%	X	12	12	A	PO Box 2933, San Antonio TX 78299 210/351-2044 www.sbc.com

Company Name/Stock Symbol	Industry	Price	P/E	YIELD	Dividend Reinvestment Plan	Year High EPS	Year High Dividend	S&P Rank	Address/Phone Number
SCANA Corp./SCG	Electric Utility	25	13.6	6.0%	X	4	45	A–	Columbia SC 29218 800/763-5891 www.scana.com
Schering-Plough Corp./SGP	Health Care	51	28.3	1.5%	X	15	11	A+	One Giralda Farms, Madison NJ 07940 201/822-7000 www.myhealth.com
Schulman, A. Inc./SHLM	Chemicals	24	19.7	1.8%		0	14	A	3550 W. Market St., Akron OH 44333 330/666-3751
SEMCO Energy Corp./SMGS	Natural Gas	17	def.	4.5%	X	0	20	A–	PO Box 5026, Port Huron MI 48061 800/225-7647 www.streetlink.com
Service Corp. International/SRV	Special Services	35	29.4	0.9%		8	23	A–	PO Box 130548, Houston TX 77219 713/522-5141
ServiceMaster L.P./SVM	Special Services	24	20.7	2.0%	X	2	27	A+	One ServiceMaster Way, Downers Grove IL 60515 630/271-1300
Sherwin-Williams Co./SHW	Bldng. Materials	32	22.5	1.2%	X	18	17	A+	101 Prospect Ave. NW, Cleveland OH 44115 216/566-2000
SIGCORP Inc./SIG	Electric Utility	26	14.3	4.5%	X	1	37	A	PO Box 3606, Evansville IN 47735 800/227-8625 www.sigcorpinc.com
Sigma-Aldrich Corp./SIAL	Chemicals	34	22.4	0.7%		26	25	A+	3050 Spruce St., St. Louis MO 63103 800/521-8956 www.sial.com/sig.aid

Company/Symbol	Industry								Address
SJW Corp./SJW(A)	Water Utility	54	12.5	4.2%		2	28	B+	374 W. Santa Clara St., San Jose CA 35196 408/279-7810 www.sjwater.com
Smucker, J.M. Co./SJMA	Foods	21	19.8	2.5%	X	1	21	A–	Strawberry Ln., Orrville OH 44667 216/682-3000
Sonoco Products Co./SON	Containers	32	18.9	2.2%	X	4	14	A–	PO Box 160, Hartsville SC 29551 803/383-7277 www.sonoco.com
Southern California Water/SCW	Water Utility	22	14.4	5.5%	X	1	43	B+	630 E. Foothill Blvd., San Dimas CA 91773 909/394-3600 www.scwater.com
SouthTrust Corp./SOTR	Banking	45	15.7	2.2%	X	17	26	A	PO Box 2554, Birmingham AL 35290 205/254-6868 www.southtrust.com
Standard Register Co./SR	Ofc. Equip./Supp.	32	14.0	2.5%		6	19	A	PO Box 1167, Dayton OH 45401 937/443-1304 www.stdreg.com
Standex International Corp./SXI	Manufacturing	29	14.8	2.7%		0	10	A	6 Manor Pkwy., Salem NH 03079 603/893-9701
Stanhome Inc./STH	Retail	33	15.4	3.4%	X	0	13	B+	Syms Way, Secaucus NJ 07094 201/902-9600
Stanley Works/SWK	Hdwre. & Tools	44	NMF	1.8%	X	0	29	B+	1000 Stanley Dr., New Britain CT 06053 860/225-5111 www.stanleyworks.com
Star Banc Corp./STB	Banking	46	23.2	1.4%	X	7	24	A+	425 Walnut St., Cincinnati OH 45202 513/632-4524 www.starbank.com

Company Name/Stock Symbol	Industry	Price	P/E	YIELD	Dividend Reinvestment Plan	Year High EPS	Year High Dividend	S&P Rank	Address/Phone Number
State Street Corp./STT	Banking	52	13.4	1.5%	X	19	18	A+	Box 351, Boston MA 02101 617/664-3477 www.statestreet.com
Stepan Co./SCL	Chemicals	26	15.1	1.9%		4	29	A–	Northfield IL 60093 847/446-7500 www.stepan.com
Stryker Corp./STRY	Medical Prods.	42	35.3	0.1%		20	4	A–	PO Box 4085, Kalamazoo MI 49003 616/385-2600
SunTrust Banks Inc./STI	Banking	61	20.8	1.5%	X	12	21	A+	PO Box 4118, Atlanta GA 30302 800/568-3476 www.SunTrust.com
Superior Industries Intl. Inc./SUP	Auto Parts	27	15.0	1.0%		0	13	A	7800 Woodley Ave., Van Nuys CA 91406 818/771-5906
Superior Surgical Mfg./SGC(A)	Textiles/Apparel	14	12.7	2.9%		1	19	B+	PO Box 4002, Seminole FL 33775 813/397-9611
Supervalu Inc./SVU	Distributor	40	15.0	2.6%	X	2	25	A–	PO Box 990, Minneapolis MN 55440 612/828-4599 www.supervalu.com
Susquehanna Bancshares/SUSQ	Banking	27	11.5	4.7%	X	2	10	A–	26 N. Cedar St., Lititz PA 17543 717/626-4721 www.susqbanc.com

Company/Symbol	Industry								Address
Synovus Financial Corp./SNV	Banking	28	31.8	1.3%	X	14	15	A+	PO Box 120, Columbus GA 31902 706/649-5220 www.snv.com
SYSCO Corp./SYY	Distributor	38	23.0	1.6%	X	20	26	A+	1390 Enclave Pkwy., Houston TX 77077 800/337-9726 www.sysco.com
TCA Cable TV Inc./TCAT	Broadcasting	40	27.4	1.6%	X	6	14	A–	PO Box 130489, Tyler TX 75713 903/595-3701
TECO Energy Inc./TE	Electric Utility	25	15.0	4.7%	X	10	37	A	PO Box 111, Tampa FL 33601 813/228-4111 www.teco.com
Teleflex Inc./TFX	Electronics	34	20.4	1.2%	X	22	19	A+	630 W. Germantown Pike, Plymouth Mtg. PA 19462 610/834-6301
Telephone & Data Sys./TDS(A)	Telephone	37	32.2	1.1%	X(5)	3	22	A–	30 N. LaSalle #4000, Chicago IL 60602 312/630-1900 www.teldta.com
Temple-Inland Inc./TIN	Containers	65	45.1	2.0%	X	0	13	B+	Drawer N, Diboll TX 75941 409/829-1313
Tennant Co./TANT	Machinery	35	15.4	2.1%	X	3	25	A–	PO Box 1452, Minneapolis MN 55440 612/540-1209
Thermo Electron Corp./TMO	Electronics	34	24.3	0.0%		12	0	B+	PO Box 9046, Waltham MA 02254 617/622-1000 www.thermo.com
Tompkins County Trustco/TMP(A)	Banking	35	13.5	3.4%	X	7	14	NA	PO Box 460, Ithaca NY 14851 607/273-3210
Tootsie Roll Industries, Inc./TR	Foods	49	22.9	0.7%		15	33	A	7401 S. Cicero Ave., Chicago IL 60629 312/838-3400
Torchmark Corp./TMK	Insurance/Life	39	17.3	1.5%	X	2	45	A+	2001 Third Ave. S., Birmingham AL 35233 205/325-4200

Company Name/Stock Symbol	Industry	Price	P/E	YIELD	Dividend Reinvestment Plan	Year High EPS	Year High Dividend	S&P Rank	Address/Phone Number
Travelers Group Inc./TRV	Insurance/Multi.	68	17.8	0.9%	X	2	10	A	388 Greenwich St., New York NY 10022
T. Rowe Price Associates/TROW	Financial	54	29.3	0.8%		6	12	A−	100 E. Pratt St., Baltimore MD 21202 410/547-2000
TRUSTCO Bank Corp NY/TRST	Banking	23	15.8	4.9%	X	21	20	NA	PO Box 1082, Schenectady NY 12301 518/381-3601
Trustmark Corp./TRMK	Banking	28	14.4	2.0%	X	5	23	A	PO Box 291, Jackson MS 39205 601/354-5111 www.trustmark.com
TRW Inc./TRW	Miscellaneous	59	35.3	2.1%	X	0	25	B+	1900 Richmond Rd., Cleveland OH 44124 216/291-7506 www.trw.com
Union Electric Co./UEP	Electric Utility	37	13.0	6.9%	X	0	21	A−	PO Box 66887, St. Louis MO 63166 800/255-2237 www.ue.com
United Asset Management/UAM	Investment Bank	28	19.9	2.6%		12	10	A+	One Intl. Pl., Boston MA 02110 617/330-8900
United Dominion Realty Trust/UDR	RE Invest. Trust	14	10.7	7.2%	X	5	20	NA	10 S. Sixth St., Richmond VA 23219 804/780-2691 www.udrt.com

Company/Symbol	Industry							Rating	Address
United Fire & Casualty Co./UFCS	Insurance/Multi.	39	20.3	1.6%		0	11	B+	PO Box 73909, Cedar Rapids IA 52407 319/399-5700
Unitil Corp./UTL(A)	Electric Utility	22	11.3	6.1%	X	4	11	A–	6 Liberty Ln. W., Hampton NH 03842 800/999-6501 www.unitil.com
Universal Corp./UVV	Tobacco	34	12.8	3.1%	X	1	26	B	PO Box 25099, Richmond VA 23260 804/254-8689
Universal Foods Corp./UFC	Foods	38	21.2	2.7%	X	0	25	A–	433 E. Michigan St., Milwaukee MI 53202 800/558-9892
U.S. Bancorp Inc./USBC	Banking	65	20.6	1.9%	X	4	39	A	601 Second Ave. So., Minneapolis MN 55402 612/332-4945 www.usbancorp.com
UST Inc./UST	Tobacco	29	12.0	5.6%	X	35	26	A+	100 W. Putnam Ave., Greenwich CT 06830 203/661-1100 www.ustshareholder.com
UtiliCorp United Inc./UCU	Electric Utility	30	11.8	5.9%	X(5)	1	39	B+	PO Box 13287, Kansas City MO 64199 800/487-6661 www.utilicorp.com
VF Corp./VFC	Textiles/Apparel	87	17.8	1.7%	X	1	25	A–	PO Box 1022, Reading PA 19603 888/836-3971 www.threads.vfc.com
Valley Resources Inc./VR(A)	Natural Gas	11	13.9	6.6%	X	1	18	A–	PO Box 7900, Cumberland RI 02864 401/334-1188
Valspar Corp./VAL	Bldng. Materials	33	24.1	1.1%		22	19	A+	PO Box 1461, Minneapolis MN 55440 612/332-7371
Wachovia Corp./WB	Banking	63	15.8	2.5%	X	5	19	A	PO Box 3099, Winston-Salem NC 27150 910/732-5787 www.wachovia.com

Company Name/Stock Symbol	Industry	Price	P/E	YIELD	Dividend Reinvestment Plan	Year High EPS	Year High Dividend	S&P Rank	Address/Phone Number
Wal-Mart Stores Inc./WMT	Retail	36	26.3	0.8%	X	35	13	A+	Bentonville AR 72716 800/438-6278 www.wal-mart.com
Walgreen Co./WAG	Retail Drug	58	34.3	0.8%	X	22	20	A+	200 Wilmot Rd., Deerfield IL 60015 847/940-2972 www.walgreens.com
Wallace Computer Services/WCS	Ofc. Equip./Supp.	33	19.0	1.7%		6	26	A	2275 Cabot Dr., Lisle IL 60532 630/588-5000
Warner-Lambert Co./WLA	Health Care	142	NMF	1.1%	X	3	44	A−	201 Tabor Rd., Morris Plains NJ 07950 201/540-2000 www.warner-lambert.com
Washington Federal Inc./WFSL	Savings & Loan	26	13.8	3.5%		1	13	A	425 Pike St., Seattle WA 98101 206/624-7930
Washington Gas Light/WGL	Natural Gas	25	15.2	4.7%	X	5	20	A	PO Box 96502, Washington DC 20078 800/221-9427
Washington REIT/WRE(A)	RE Invest. Trust	17	14.7	6.4%	X	31	26	NA	10400 Connecticut Ave., Kensington MD 20895 800/565-9748 www.shareholdernews.com
Wausau Paper Mills Inc./WSAU	Paper/Forest	20	17.5	1.2%	X	1	13	A−	PO Box 1408, Wausau WI 54402 715/845-5266

Company/Symbol	Industry								Address
WD-40 Co./WDFC	Chemicals	60	44.1	2.1%		2	22	B+	1061 Cudahy Place, San Diego CA 92110 619/275-1400
Weingarten Realty Investors/WRI	RE Invest. Trust	43	13.7	6.0%	X	7	12	NA	PO Box 924133, Houston TX 77292 713/866-6000 www.weingarten.com
Weis Markets Inc./WMK	Grocery	31	16.8	3.1%	X	4	31	A−	1000 S. Second St., Sunbury PA 17801 717/286-4571
Wesco Financial Corp./WSC(A)	Financial	270	62.8	0.4%		0	25	B+	315 E. Colorado Blvd., Pasadena CA 91101 818/585-6700
Western Resources Inc./WR	Electric Utility	34	14.4	6.2%	X	0	21	B+	PO Box 750320, Topeka KS 66675 800/527-2495 www.wstnres.com
Weyco Group Inc./WEYS	Shoes	73	41.0	0.4%		3	16	NA	PO Box 1188, Milwaukee WI 53201 414/263-8800
WICOR Inc./WIC	Natural Gas	39	16.2	4.4%	X	4	13	B+	626 E Wisconsin Ave., Milwaukee WI 53202 800/236-3453 www.investquest.com
Wilmington Trust Corp./WILM	Banking	47	15.7	3.1%	X	15	15	A+	Rodney Square N., Wilmington DE 19890 800/441-7120
Winn-Dixie Stores Inc./WIN	Grocery	38	25.3	2.7%	X	2	53	A+	PO Box B, Jacksonville FL 32203 888/822-5593
Wisconsin Energy Corp./WEC	Electric Utility	25	13.9	6.2%	X	0	36	A−	PO Box 2949, Milwaukee WI 53201 800/558-9663 www.wisenergy.com
Worthington Industries/WTHG	Steel	19	19.6	2.7%	X	0	28	B+	1205 Dearborn Dr., Columbus OH 43085 614/438-3210

Company Name/ Stock Symbol	Industry	Price	P/E	YIELD	Dividend Reinvestment Plan	Year High EPS	Year High Dividend	S&P Rank	Address/Phone Number
WPL Holdings Inc./WPH	Electric Utility	27	13.1	7.4%	X	4	24	A	PO Box 2568, Madison WI 53701 800/356-5343 www.wplh.com
WPS Resources Corp./ WPS	Electric Utility	28	15.7	6.9%	X	0	38	B+	PO Box 19001, Green Bay WI 54307 800/236-1551 www.wpst.com
Wrigley, Wm. Jr. Co./ WWY	Foods	72	35.5	1.5%	X	15	16	A+	410 N. Michigan Ave., Chicago IL 60611 800/824-9681 www.wrigley.com
York Financial/YFED	Savings & Loan	21	22.1	2.9%	X(10)	2	10	B+	101 S. George St., York PA 17401 717/846-8777

INDEX

INDEX

Graham, Benjamin, 14, 37–45, 114
  on common stocks, 41–42
  on financial professionals, 42, 44,
    84–85
  on forecasting, 44
  on individual investor's advantage,
    42–43, 44, 68, 84–85
  investing rules of, 43, 44–45
  and P/E ratios, 199
  on quality of stocks, 50
  on security analysis, 43, 47
  on stock-picking, 43
Gray, Florence, 4–5
Great Crash of 1987, 76
Great Depression, 4, 36, 71, 112, 120–21
Green, Hetty, 90–91
growth:
  and dividends, 168–69
  long-term, 26
  yields vs., 168 60
guaranteed investment contracts (GICs),
    102, 103, 104

Hack, Ed, 5
Haisley, Paul, 106
Henry, Patrick, 26
Hermundslie, Palmer J., 58
history, 18–32
  brokers in, 19–20
  of compound interest, 32–34
  of New York Stock Exchange, 20–21
  of stocks, 18–22, 26
Hoffer, Eric, 74
Hoover, Herbert, 71
housing, 31, 32
Hulbert, Mark, 65
Hulbert's Financial Digest, 65

Ibbotson Associates, 63
individual investors, 110–52
  confidence lacking in, 68
  financial professionals vs., 42–43,
    60–85
  Graham on, 42–43, 44, 68, 84–85
  and IRAs, 104–6
  and market indexes, 67
  in New York Stock Exchange, 67
  retirement plans of, 104; see also
    retirement plans
individual retirement accounts (IRAs),
    104–6, 107
industry categories, 197
inflation:
  in future, 30, 32

  and money-market funds, 30
  and retirement plans, 97–100, 103
  and returns, 29
  and Rule of 72, 97
institutional funds, see financial
    professionals
Intelligent Investor, The (Graham), 40, 50
international stock exchanges, 21–22
Introduction to Risk and Return from
    Common Stocks, An (Brealey), 125
invest, origin of word, 2
Investment counselors, see financial
    professionals
investments:
  allocation of funds in, 127–46, 170
  basic program of, 117
  criteria for, 10–11
  fees and costs of, see commissions;
    transaction costs
  fixed income, 28 20
  getting started in, 3–4, 117, 149–52,
    197
  Graham's rules for, 43, 44–45
  guaranteed investment contracts, 102,
    103, 104
  by individuals, see individual investors
  long-term, see long term, investment
    for
  lump-sum, 116–17
  return on, see returns
  safety of, 14, 30, 39, 50
  simplicity of, 46–59
  stocks as, see stocks
  and taxes, see taxes
  by young people, 180–88; see also
    young people
  see also money management; portfolios
investment trusts, 61–62
IRAs (individual retirement accounts),
    104–6, 107

Jack White & Co., 174
Johnson, Theodore, 94
Jones, Edward D., 25
Junior Achievement (JA), 93, 186

Kennedy Cabot, 176–77, 186
Keogh plans, 107–8
Keynes, John Maynard, 125
Kiplinger's Personal Finance Magazine,
    66, 81–82
Knight, Charles (Chuck), 55–56

Lao-tzu, 75
Levine, Leon, 167

251

INDEX

ou are invited to join "The Staton Institute℠ **– America's Finest Investors**®**" at a Spectacular Savings.**

As our way of thanking you for buying this copy of "The America's Finest Companies® Investment Plan," please consider this your Personal Invitation to become a Member of "The Staton Institute℠ – America's Finest Investors®" at the <u>Special Rock-Bottom Bargain Introductory Rate</u> of *only $99, which includes* a one-year subscription to *The Staton Institute*℠ *Advisory* ($117/yr.) and a number of other wealthbuilding materials totaling $231.80. Yours for just $99.

Call toll free 800/779-7175 or clip and mail to The Staton Institute℠ Inc., 300 East Blvd. B-4, Charlotte, NC 28203. Or fax this coupon to 704/332-0427. You can also visit our Web site at www.StatonInstitute.com

☐ YES, I want to become a Member of "The Staton Institute℠ – America's Finest Investors®."

Name _____ Title _____
          (please print legibly)

Firm _____

Address _____

City/State /ZIP _____

Daytime Phone (____) _____ FAX (____) _____

E-Mail Address _____

The Staton Institute℠**First-Year Membership**	**$99.00**

	NC Residents Add 6% Tax	**5.94**
☐ Check enclosed for $ _____	Shipping & Handling	**6.95**
☐ Charge to my credit card	Foreign Orders add US $20	
☐ VISA ☐ M/CARD ☐ AMEX Exp. Date _____	TOTAL	

Signature _____   97HY-1

Do Your Friends and Colleagues a Favor by Giving Them a **FREE** Copy of "The Staton Institute^{SM} Advisory."

So many people have benefited from the valuable insights and advice contained in each monthly issue of "The Staton Institute^{SM} Advisory" you will be doing your friends, relatives, colleagues – and yourself – a real favor if you send us their names so we can mail a no-obligation sample issue.

It will be sent FREE with your compliments.

And, "yes" we will be glad to send you a FREE copy of this newsletter so you can see for yourself just how useful Bill Staton's plain-English advice can be. There's no limit to the number of names you can send. Just be sure you submit a complete address in a legible way.

Your Name _____
          (please print legibly)

Address _____

City/State/ZIP_____

Daytime Phone (_____)_____ Fax (_____)_____

E-Mail Address_____

Initial here _____ *if you want a no obligation free sample issue of the "Advisory" for yourself.*

At no-obligation, send FREE sample issue of the "Advisory" newsletter to:

Name _____
      (please print legibly)

Address _____

City/State/ZIP_____

Write below how you want each "gift notice" to read:

From: _____

Mail to "Sample Newsletter" c/o The Staton Institute^{SM}, 300 East Blvd. B-4, Charlotte, NC 28203 or fax 704/332-0427. Visit our web site at www.StatonInstitute.com